JOHN
F.
KENNEDY

JOHN F. KENNEDY

Marta Randall

CHELSEA HOUSE PUBLISHERS
NEW YORK
PHILADELPHIA

EDITOR-IN-CHIEF: Nancy Toff
EXECUTIVE EDITOR: Remmel T. Nunn
MANAGING EDITOR: Karyn Gullen Browne
COPY CHIEF: Juliann Barbato
ART DIRECTOR: Giannella G. Garrett
PICTURE EDITOR: Adrian Allen
MANUFACTURING MANAGER: Gerald Levine

Staff for JOHN F. KENNEDY:

SENIOR EDITOR: John W. Selfridge
ASSISTANT EDITORS: Pierre Hauser, Kathleen McDermott, Bert Yaeger
EDITORIAL ASSISTANT: James Guiry
COPY EDITORS: Gillian Bucky, Sean Dolan, Michael Goodman, Ellen Scordato
ASSISTANT DESIGNER: Jill Goldreyer
PICTURE RESEARCH: Elie Porter
SENIOR DESIGNER: David Murray
PRODUCTION COORDINATOR: Laura McCormick
COVER ILLUSTRATION: Alan Nahigian

Frontispiece courtesy of UPI/BETTMANN NEWSPHOTOS

15 14 13 12 11 10

Library of Congress Cataloging in Publication Data

Randall, Marta. JOHN FITZGERALD KENNEDY

(World leaders past & present)
Bibliography: p.
Includes index.
1. Kennedy, John F. (John Fitzgerald), 1917–1963—
Juvenile literature. 2. Presidents—United States—
Biography—Juvenile literature. 3. United States—Politics
and government—1961–1963—Juvenile literature.
[1. Kennedy, John F. (John Fitzgerald), 1917–1963.
2. Presidents. 3. United States—History—1961–1969]
I. Title. II. Series: World leaders past & present.
E842.Z9R36   1988   973.922'092'4 [B] [92] 87-14595

ISBN 0-87754-586-3
    0-7910-0580-1 (pbk.)

Contents

John Adams
John Quincy Adams
Konrad Adenauer
Alexander the Great
Salvador Allende
Marc Antony
Corazon Aquino
Yasir Arafat
King Arthur
Hafez al-Assad
Kemal Atatürk
Attila
Clement Attlee
Augustus Caesar
Menachem Begin
David Ben-Gurion
Otto von Bismarck
Léon Blum
Simon Bolívar
Cesare Borgia
Willy Brandt
Leonid Brezhnev
Julius Caesar
John Calvin
Jimmy Carter
Fidel Castro
Catherine the Great
Charlemagne
Chiang Kai-Shek
Winston Churchill
Georges Clemenceau
Cleopatra
Constantine the Great
Hernán Cortés
Oliver Cromwell
Georges-Jacques
   Danton
Jefferson Davis
Moshe Dayan
Charles de Gaulle
Eamon De Valera
Eugene Debs
Deng Xiaoping
Benjamin Disraeli
Alexander Dubček
François & Jean-Claude
   Duvalier
Dwight Eisenhower
Eleanor of Aquitaine
Elizabeth i
Faisal
Ferdinand & Isabella
Francisco Franco
Benjamin Franklin

Frederick the Great
Indira Gandhi
Mohandas Gandhi
Giuseppe Garibaldi
Amin & Bashir Gemayel
Genghis Khan
William Gladstone
Mikhail Gorbachev
Ulysses S. Grant
Ernesto "Che" Guevara
Tenzin Gyatso
Alexander Hamilton
Dag Hammarskjöld
Henry viii
Henry of Navarre
Paul von Hindenburg
Hirohito
Adolf Hitler
Ho Chi Minh
King Hussein
Ivan the Terrible
Andrew Jackson
James i
Wojciech Jaruzelski
Thomas Jefferson
Joan of Arc
Pope John xxiii
Pope John Paul ii
Lyndon Johnson
Benito Juárez
John Kennedy
Robert Kennedy
Jomo Kenyatta
Ayatollah Khomeini
Nikita Khrushchev
Kim Il Sung
Martin Luther King, Jr.
Henry Kissinger
Kublai Khan
Lafayette
Robert E. Lee
Vladimir Lenin
Abraham Lincoln
David Lloyd George
Louis xiv
Martin Luther
Judas Maccabeus
James Madison
Nelson & Winnie
   Mandela
Mao Zedong
Ferdinand Marcos
George Marshall

Mary, Queen of Scots
Tomáš Masaryk
Golda Meir
Klemens von Metternich
James Monroe
Hosni Mubarak
Robert Mugabe
Benito Mussolini
Napoléon Bonaparte
Gamal Abdel Nasser
Jawaharlal Nehru
Nero
Nicholas II
Richard Nixon
Kwame Nkrumah
Daniel Ortega
Mohammed Reza Pahlavi
Thomas Paine
Charles Stewart
   Parnell
Pericles
Juan Perón
Peter the Great
Pol Pot
Muammar el-Qaddafi
Ronald Reagan
Cardinal Richelieu
Maximilien Robespierre
Eleanor Roosevelt
Franklin Roosevelt
Theodore Roosevelt
Anwar Sadat
Haile Selassie
Prince Sihanouk
Jan Smuts
Joseph Stalin
Sukarno
Sun Yat-sen
Tamerlane
Mother Teresa
Margaret Thatcher
Josip Broz Tito
Toussaint L'Ouverture
Leon Trotsky
Pierre Trudeau
Harry Truman
Queen Victoria
Lech Walesa
George Washington
Chaim Weizmann
Woodrow Wilson
Xerxes
Emiliano Zapata
Zhou Enlai

CHELSEA HOUSE PUBLISHERS

ON LEADERSHIP
Arthur M. Schlesinger, jr.

LEADERSHIP, it may be said, is really what makes the world go round. Love no doubt smooths the passage; but love is a private transaction between consenting adults. Leadership is a public transaction with history. The idea of leadership affirms the capacity of individuals to move, inspire, and mobilize masses of people so that they act together in pursuit of an end. Sometimes leadership serves good purposes, sometimes bad; but whether the end is benign or evil, great leaders are those men and women who leave their personal stamp on history.

Now, the very concept of leadership implies the proposition that individuals can make a difference. This proposition has never been universally accepted. From classical times to the present day, eminent thinkers have regarded individuals as no more than the agents and pawns of larger forces, whether the gods and goddesses of the ancient world or, in the modern era, race, class, nation, the dialectic, the will of the people, the spirit of the times, history itself. Against such forces, the individual dwindles into insignificance.

So contends the thesis of historical determinism. Tolstoy's great novel *War and Peace* offers a famous statement of the case. Why, Tolstoy asked, did millions of men in the Napoleonic wars, denying their human feelings and their common sense, move back and forth across Europe slaughtering their fellows? "The war," Tolstoy answered, "was bound to happen simply because it was bound to happen." All prior history predetermined it. As for leaders, they, Tolstoy said, "are but the labels that serve to give a name to an end and, like labels, they have the least possible connection with the event." The greater the leader, "the more conspicuous the inevitability and the predestination of every act he commits." The leader, said Tolstoy, is "the slave of history."

Determinism takes many forms. Marxism is the determinism of class. Nazism the determinism of race. But the idea of men and women as the slaves of history runs athwart the deepest human instincts. Rigid determinism abolishes the idea of human freedom—

the assumption of free choice that underlies every move we make, every word we speak, every thought we think. It abolishes the idea of human responsibility, since it is manifestly unfair to reward or punish people for actions that are by definition beyond their control. No one can live consistently by any deterministic creed. The Marxist states prove this themselves by their extreme susceptibility to the cult of leadership.

More than that, history refutes the idea that individuals make no difference. In December 1931 a British politician crossing Park Avenue in New York City between 76th and 77th Streets around 10:30 P.M. looked in the wrong direction and was knocked down by an automobile—a moment, he later recalled, of a man aghast, a world aglare: "I do not understand why I was not broken like an eggshell or squashed like a gooseberry." Fourteen months later an American politician, sitting in an open car in Miami, Florida, was fired on by an assassin; the man beside him was hit. Those who believe that individuals make no difference to history might well ponder whether the next two decades would have been the same had Mario Constasino's car killed Winston Churchill in 1931 and Giuseppe Zangara's bullet killed Franklin Roosevelt in 1933. Suppose, in addition, that Adolf Hitler had been killed in the street fighting during the Munich *Putsch* of 1923 and that Lenin had died of typhus during World War I. What would the 20th century be like now?

For better or for worse, individuals do make a difference. "The notion that a people can run itself and its affairs anonymously," wrote the philosopher William James, "is now well known to be the silliest of absurdities. Mankind does nothing save through initiatives on the part of inventors, great or small, and imitation by the rest of us—these are the sole factors in human progress. Individuals of genius show the way, and set the patterns, which common people then adopt and follow."

Leadership, James suggests, means leadership in thought as well as in action. In the long run, leaders in thought may well make the greater difference to the world. But, as Woodrow Wilson once said, "Those only are leaders of men, in the general eye, who lead in action. . . . It is at their hands that new thought gets its translation into the crude language of deeds." Leaders in thought often invent in solitude and obscurity, leaving to later generations the tasks of imitation. Leaders in action—the leaders portrayed in this series—have to be effective in their own time.

And they cannot be effective by themselves. They must act in response to the rhythms of their age. Their genius must be adapted, in a phrase of William James's, "to the receptivities of the moment." Leaders are useless without followers. "There goes the mob," said the French politician hearing a clamor in the streets. "I am their leader. I must follow them." Great leaders turn the inchoate emotions of the mob to purposes of their own. They seize on the opportunities of their time, the hopes, fears, frustrations, crises, potentialities. They succeed when events have prepared the way for them, when the community is awaiting to be aroused, when they can provide the clarifying and organizing ideas. Leadership ignites the circuit between the individual and the mass and thereby alters history.

It may alter history for better or for worse. Leaders have been responsible for the most extravagant follies and most monstrous crimes that have beset suffering humanity. They have also been vital in such gains as humanity has made in individual freedom, religious and racial tolerance, social justice and respect for human rights.

There is no sure way to tell in advance who is going to lead for good and who for evil. But a glance at the gallery of men and women in *World Leaders—Past and Present* suggests some useful tests.

One test is this: do leaders lead by force or by persuasion? By command or by consent? Through most of history leadership was exercised by the divine right of authority. The duty of followers was to defer and to obey. "Theirs not to reason why,/ Theirs but to do and die." On occasion, as with the so-called "enlightened despots" of the 18th century in Europe, absolutist leadership was animated by humane purposes. More often, absolutism nourished the passion for domination, land, gold and conquest and resulted in tyranny.

The great revolution of modern times has been the revolution of equality. The idea that all people should be equal in their legal condition has undermined the old structure of authority, hierarchy and deference. The revolution of equality has had two contrary effects on the nature of leadership. For equality, as Alexis de Tocqueville pointed out in his great study *Democracy in America*, might mean equality in servitude as well as equality in freedom.

"I know of only two methods of establishing equality in the political world," Tocqueville wrote. "Rights must be given to every citizen, or none at all to anyone . . . save one, who is the master of all." There was no middle ground "between the sovereignty of all and the absolute power of one man." In his astonishing prediction of 20th-century totalitarian dictatorship, Tocqueville explained how the revolution of equality could lead to the *"Führerprinzip"* and more terrible absolutism than the world had ever known.

But when rights are given to every citizen and the sovereignty of all is established, the problem of leadership takes a new form, becomes more exacting than ever before. It is easy to issue commands and enforce them by the rope and the stake, the concentration camp and the *gulag.* It is much harder to use argument and achievement to overcome opposition and win consent. The Founding Fathers of the United States understood the difficulty. They believed that history had given them the opportunity to decide, as Alexander Hamilton wrote in the first Federalist Paper, whether men are indeed capable of basing government on "reflection and choice, or whether they are forever destined to depend . . . on accident and force."

Government by reflection and choice called for a new style of leadership and a new quality of followership. It required leaders to be responsive to popular concerns, and it required followers to be active and informed participants in the process. Democracy does not eliminate emotion from politics; sometimes it fosters demagoguery; but it is confident that, as the greatest of democratic leaders put it, you cannot fool all of the people all of the time. It measures leadership by results and retires those who overreach or falter or fail.

It is true that in the long run despots are measured by results too. But they can postpone the day of judgment, sometimes indefinitely, and in the meantime they can do infinite harm. It is also true that democracy is no guarantee of virtue and intelligence in government, for the voice of the people is not necessarily the voice of God. But democracy, by assuring the right of opposition, offers built-in resistance to the evils inherent in absolutism. As the theologian Reinhold Niebuhr summed it up, "Man's capacity for justice makes democracy possible, but man's inclination to injustice makes democracy necessary."

A second test for leadership is the end for which power is sought. When leaders have as their goal the supremacy of a master race or the promotion of totalitarian revolution or the acquisition and exploitation of colonies or the protection of greed and privilege or the preservation of personal power, it is likely that their leadership will do little to advance the cause of humanity. When their goal is the abolition of slavery, the liberation of women, the enlargement of opportunity for the poor and powerless, the extension of equal rights to racial minorities, the defense of the freedoms of expression and opposition, it is likely that their leadership will increase the sum of human liberty and welfare.

Leaders have done great harm to the world. They have also conferred great benefits. You will find both sorts in this series. Even "good" leaders must be regarded with a certain wariness. Leaders are not demigods; they put on their trousers one leg after another just like ordinary mortals. No leader is infallible, and every leader needs to be reminded of this at regular intervals. Irreverence irritates leaders but is their salvation. Unquestioning submission corrupts leaders and demands followers. Making a cult of a leader is always a mistake. Fortunately hero worship generates its own antidote. "Every hero," said Emerson, "becomes a bore at last."

The signal benefit the great leaders confer is to embolden the rest of us to live according to our own best selves, to be active, insistent, and resolute in affirming our own sense of things. For great leaders attest to the reality of human freedom against the supposed inevitabilities of history. And they attest to the wisdom and power that may lie within the most unlikely of us, which is why Abraham Lincoln remains the supreme example of great leadership. A great leader, said Emerson, exhibits new possibilities to all humanity. "We feed on genius. . . . Great men exist that there may be greater men."

Great leaders, in short, justify themselves by emancipating and empowering their followers. So humanity struggles to master its destiny, remembering with Alexis de Tocqueville: "It is true that around every man a fatal circle is traced beyond which he cannot pass; but within the wide verge of that circle he is powerful and free; as it is with man, so with communities."

1
A Warm, Clear Day in Dallas

On November 22, 1963, at 12:30 in the afternoon, a man with a rifle crouched behind a window in the Texas School Book Depository above Dealey Plaza in Dallas, Texas.

It was a clear, brilliant autumn day, and the crowds in the street below cheered and waved as President John F. Kennedy's limousine passed by. The president and his wife, Jacqueline, smiled and waved back; earlier the president had stopped the motorcade twice, once to shake hands with a little girl, and a second time to greet a Catholic nun and her group of school children. During both of these stops, the Secret Service worked frantically to keep the crowd at a distance. Dallas, with a murder rate twice the national average and a vocal and hostile anti-Kennedy element, was not a safe city. Just a day earlier the city had been covered with hate posters and leaflets denouncing the president. That morning's *Dallas News* had carried a full-page advertisement criticizing Kennedy for his abandonment of the Constitution and softness toward Moscow and communism. But this afternoon the crowd seemed friendly, and the president wanted to be close to the people, to touch their hands and talk with them.

Now he is a legend when he would have preferred to be a man.
—JACQUELINE KENNEDY former first lady, on her husband, John F. Kennedy, 1964

A crowd at Love Airport in Dallas, Texas, anticipates the arrival of President John F. Kennedy and his entourage on November 22, 1963. Despite warnings, Kennedy was unconcerned for his own safety that day and refused to use a protective shield atop the presidential limousine.

Jacqueline Kennedy, her dress splattered with blood following the assassination of her husband, watches as the president's body is taken to Bethesda Naval Hospital, Maryland. Attorney General Robert Kennedy, the president's brother, stands to the left of the first lady.

The day before, he had visited the Texas cities of San Antonio, Houston, and Fort Worth, and in all three cities he had been greeted enthusiastically. When Air Force One, the president's plane, arrived in Dallas, a crowd of about 4,000 people was there to greet him. He took time to walk along the security barrier and shake hands and talk with them.

Though it was hoped that the greatest disturbance in Dallas would be shouts from an unfriendly crowd, the Secret Service, responsible for protecting the president, had identified potentially dangerous groups in Dallas: Cubans upset at the president's handling of the uneasy relationship between the United States and Cuba, racists angry at Kennedy's strong support of civil rights legislation, conservatives who believed the president was soft on communism, radicals who believed the president was not soft enough on communism, and others. A few weeks earlier, Adlai Stevenson, the U.S. delegate to the United Nations, had been heckled, spat upon, and hit with a placard by an unruly group of demonstrators. Always cautious, the Secret Service wanted Kennedy to use a protective bubble-top over the open limousine, but so far the president had met only friendly and happy people in Texas, and he was not overly concerned. The president ordered that the bubble-top not be used.

The motorcade entered Main Street and approached Dealey Plaza. Texas Governor John Connally and his wife, Nellie, were riding in the limousine with the president, and Mrs. Connally said, "Mr. President, you can't say Dallas doesn't love you." The president waved at the crowd and said, "That's obvious." It seemed to be true.

John F. Kennedy had been president for a little more than a thousand days, and in that time he had brought the country through crises that shook the world. From the early humiliation of a badly planned and disastrous invasion of Cuba, he had gone on to challenge the nuclear might of the Soviet Union over missile bases in Cuba, confronted the Soviet Union over the explosive issue of the Berlin Wall, founded an Alliance for Progress that knit together the United States and Latin America, committed the United States to outer space exploration, and signed a nuclear test ban treaty with the Soviet Union and other countries. Perhaps the most important of his achievements was his support for civil rights and his effort to move the United States away from racial segregation and toward freedom and equal rights for all Americans. Kennedy called his program "the New Frontier"; he emphasized fresh solutions to the new, increasingly complex problems faced by the United States. Though he demanded hard work from himself, his staff, and all Americans, his youth, intellectual vigor, and spirit of practical optimism imbued many Americans with the belief that real progress could be made toward creating a better, more just society. Some people compared the Kennedy White House with Camelot, the idyllic court of King Arthur, the legendary Celtic king, where for "one brief, shining moment" the strongest and most virtuous knights had gathered. Like the heroic King Arthur and his beautiful queen, Guinevere, the Kennedys were young, attractive, charismatic. There was an exuberant can-do vitality about his presidential leadership and in

Lee Harvey Oswald, a 24-year-old former marine, allegedly shot President John Kennedy from a window in the Texas School Book Depository, above Dealey Plaza, Dallas. Whether Oswald acted alone or as part of a conspiracy was never determined beyond a doubt.

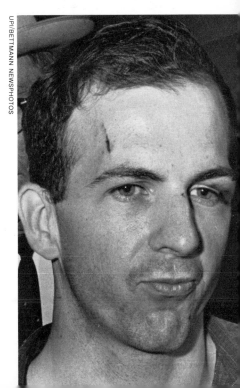

Jack Ruby, a Dallas night-club owner, slays alleged Kennedy assassin Lee Harvey Oswald as Oswald is transferred from city to county jail. Despite numerous investigative reports, many crucial questions surrounding the Kennedy assassination still remain unanswered.

her artistic and cultural renovation of the White House. As King Arthur had been advised by his knights' Round Table, Kennedy gathered around him the best and brightest people he could find — from politics, industry, the universities — to help him.

Not everyone was pleased with Kennedy and his administration, and segregation and U.S.-Soviet relations were both controversial subjects in Texas. But as the motorcade rolled on, the president was not worried. As he passed out of the sight of the people in Dealey Plaza, the man in the sixth-floor window of the Texas School Book Depository aimed his rifle and fired.

Kennedy was hit first in the throat; the second bullet shattered his skull. Governor Connally was shot through the back. Jacqueline Kennedy cried, "Oh no, no . . . Oh, my God, they have shot my husband," and held the president tightly. As the two women cradled their husbands, the limousine pulled out of the motorcade and rushed to Parkland Hospital. Mrs. Connally later recalled ". . . we must have been a horrible sight flying down the freeway with those dying men in our arms. There was no screaming in that horrible car. It was just a silent, terrible drive."

UPI/BETTMANN NEWSPHOTOS

Jacqueline Kennedy kneels at her husband's grave at Arlington National Cemetery, Virginia. Leaders from 92 countries attended the president's funeral, and more than 4 million people lined the streets to pay their respects.

At one o'clock, the president was pronounced dead; an hour and a half later, aboard Air Force One, Vice-president Lyndon Johnson was sworn in as the 36th president of the United States. Jacqueline Kennedy stood beside him, still wearing her blood-soaked suit.

At 2:15 that afternoon, a young man named Lee Harvey Oswald was arrested for the murder of John Kennedy; two days later, on national television, Oswald was shot to death by a Dallas nightclub owner named Jack Ruby. One of President Johnson's first acts in office was to create a commission headed by Earl Warren, chief justice of the Supreme Court, to investigate Kennedy's assassination. Despite the commission's finding that Oswald worked alone in killing the president, many people still believe that the assassination was the result of a conspiracy. It is likely that there will never be an explanation that satisfies everyone.

John Kennedy was buried in Arlington National Cemetery on November 25, 1963. Leaders from 92 countries attended the funeral and millions of people lined the route. Jacqueline lit an eternal flame over his grave while his two young children looked on.

Historian Herbert S. Parmet has written: "Few deaths have ever shocked so much of the world." People everywhere reacted with disbelief, shock, and grief. Jimmy Carter, a Georgia farmer who later became president of the United States, said, "I wept openly for the first time in ten years, for the first time since my own father died." Businesses and schools closed as American daily life virtually came to a halt. For four days, until the president was buried, people huddled around television sets and radios in grief and disbelief. In Copenhagen, Denmark, thousands of people brought flowers to the U.S. Embassy, so many that by the next morning the building was surrounded by flowers six feet deep. In West Berlin, people placed lit candles in darkened windows. Almost any American born before 1957 can remember where she or he was the day John Kennedy died.

Less than two hours after Kennedy was pronounced dead, Lyndon Johnson was sworn in as president of the United States. One of Johnson's first acts as president was to create a commission to investigate the Kennedy assassination.

UPI/BETTMANN NEWSPHOTOS

No president is ever popular with everyone, and John Kennedy was no exception. It is always shocking when a leader is murdered, particularly in the United States, which has seen relatively few political assassinations. But as Harold Macmillan of Great Britain wondered, speaking of the assassination: "Why was this feeling — this sorrow — at once so universal and so individual? Was it not because he seemed, in his own person, to embody all the hopes and aspirations of this new world that is struggling to emerge — to rise, Phoenix-like, from the ashes of the old?"

Who was this young American president, whose death so touched the world and the country? He had been in office for only 1,037 days, yet those days profoundly changed America and the world.

Headlines announce what most of the United States had already seen on television. There are few Americans born before 1957 who do not remember where they were or what they were doing on the day Kennedy was shot.

2

The Boy Who Would Not Be President

John Fitzgerald Kennedy was not only the youngest man ever elected president, but also the first American of Irish descent and the first Roman Catholic to serve as president. This cultural heritage exerted a strong influence on his ambitions, intellectual development, and career. To understand John Kennedy, it is important to understand his background.

Patrick Kennedy, from County Wexford, Ireland, arrived in Boston in 1849 as part of the great wave of Irish immigration to America. In Ireland the Irish potato crop had failed: deprived of their staple food, nearly 1 million Irish died of starvation and disease. More than a million more left Ireland for America. The immigrants came over on sailing ships that were so crowded and dirty that about 20 percent of them died before they reached the New World.

Like most new immigrant groups, the "famine Irish" faced discrimination and hatred in their new home. For the most part, they could find only low-paying manual labor: building railroad tracks, heav-

> *Jack Kennedy was born to public service . . . all the careers he contemplated at all seriously — law, a university presidency, politics — involved that sense of duty to mold others, a matter of noblesse oblige.*
> —HERBERT S. PARMET
> historian

Joseph Patrick Kennedy and Rose Fitzgerald on their wedding day in 1914. Though Joseph Kennedy, at the age of 26, had become the youngest bank president in the country, Rose Fitzgerald's father, a powerful Boston politician, found Kennedy unsuitable for his daughter.

Joseph Kennedy, John Kennedy's father, was the son of a Massachusetts state senator. Soon after graduating from Harvard University, Joseph Kennedy became president of the Columbia Trust Company, where his father was a director.

ing coal, digging canals, or clearing swamps. The famine Irish were Catholics, and this, too, was a cause for discrimination in the United States, where most people were Protestant. In Boston, particularly the upper classes, the so-called Brahmins, were almost exclusively Protestant; it was difficult for any Irish to enter the ranks of the social elite.

Upon arriving in America it cost two pennies to take the ferry from Noddle's Island (also called East Boston) where the ships docked, to the mainland. Like many of the famine Irish, Patrick Kennedy did not have the money for the fare and stayed in the crowded tenements of the island. He married Bridget Murphy, whom he had met on the long voyage from Ireland. They had three daughters and one son. After working as a dockhand, he became a cooper, making yokes, staves, and whiskey barrels. Nine years after his arrival, Patrick died of cholera at the age of 35.

After his death, Bridget took a job in a small shop, which she bought after she was able to save enough money. When Patrick Joseph, her son, grew up, he also saved his money and bought two saloons and a liquor-importing business. By this time the Irish immigrants and their descendants had begun to show a marked aptitude for electoral politics, particularly as practiced in the wards of the larger cities, such as Boston and New York. Patrick Joseph entered Boston politics and served three terms in the Massachusetts Senate. He married Mary Augusta Hickey, and in 1888 they had a son, Joseph Patrick, John Kennedy's father.

Joseph Kennedy was born with determination and a knack for making money. He entered Harvard University at a time when the Irish were often called "untouchables" behind their backs and was repeatedly stung by his rejection by the university's more prestigious clubs, which were dominated by the Brahmins. Joseph Kennedy attributed his rejection to his Irishness, and it fueled his determination to achieve power and prominence for himself and his family. By the time he graduated in 1912, he had begun to accumulate his fortune and was determined to become a millionaire. In 1913 he engineered a takeover of the Columbia Trust Company, becoming the youngest bank president in the country. The next year he married Rose Fitzgerald, the daughter of a colorful politician, John Fitzgerald. Known as "Honey Fitz," Fitzgerald was a fixture in Boston politics, having served a number of terms as mayor. Later he would be elected to the U.S. House of Representatives. Joseph and his wife had nine children. The oldest son, Joseph Patrick, Jr., was born in 1915. John, known as Jack, was born on May 29, 1917; the other children were Rosemary (who was retarded), Kathleen, Eunice, Patricia, Robert, Jean, and Edward.

This background shaped the entire Kennedy clan, molding them into an ambitious and competitive family who were fiercely loyal to each other and who never took "no" for an answer. Joseph Kennedy wanted winners, in school, in sports, in politics, and in business, and he had no time for losers.

It was easy for Joe, Jr., the oldest son, to be a winner; Joe was brave, daring, and self-confident, a good athlete and student. Being a winner was more difficult for Jack. Unlike his older brother, he was a sickly child, born with a weak back and plagued by childhood illnesses that included scarlet fever and a mysterious sickness that followed him throughout his life. A "blood condition," it was variously diagnosed as leukemia, jaundice, and hepatitis. As a result of his frequent illnesses, Jack spent much of his time in bed reading histories and novels, but when he played, he played hard. Of all the Kennedy children, only Jack consistently challenged his older brother in rough games and sports. Although he usually lost and was often hurt, he kept trying. For the next 20 years, Jack would find himself always in his older brother's shadow.

Jack attended several private schools and was finally enrolled at Choate, a very conservative preparatory school in Wallingford, Connecticut. Despite his poor health and thin build, he played on the Choate football team, as Joe, Jr., had done. Like his brother, Jack was popular with his classmates. Less serious than Joe, Jr., his irrepressible sense of fun and high spirits won him many friends.

Joe was the star of the family. He did everything better than the rest of us.
—JOHN F. KENNEDY
on his older brother,
Joseph P. Kennedy, Jr.

His grades did not keep up with his taste for mischief, and his academic record was poor compared to Joe, Jr.'s. He earned a reputation as a prankster, and in his final year at Choate he was voted "most likely to succeed" — because he and his friends had rigged the election.

Jack attended Princeton briefly in 1935, but health problems forced him to leave before finishing the semester. After a two-month stay in a Boston hospital he spent the remainder of his freshman year recuperating and working on a ranch near Tucson, Arizona. In the fall of 1936 he enrolled at Harvard, where Joe, Jr., had again preceded him by two years. His grades were initially undistinguished, though he impressed some of his professors with his writing and analytical abilities. Once again he played football, until a ruptured spinal disk sustained during practice forced him to leave the team. Back pain was to plague him for the rest of his life.

A Kennedy family portrait taken in 1937. Seated at extreme left and right are Joseph and Rose Kennedy. Their children, pictured left to right, are Patricia, John, Jean, Eunice, Robert, Kathleen, Edward, Rosemary, and Joseph.

In late 1937, while Jack was still at Harvard, President Franklin D. Roosevelt appointed Joseph, Sr., to be the U.S. ambassador to Great Britain. He had earlier served as the first chairman of the newly created Securities and Exchange Commission and then as head of the U.S. Maritime Commission. By 1938 the growing military strength and aggressive expansionism of Adolf Hitler's Nazi Germany had brought Europe to the brink of war. The memory of World War I, which had devastated Europe just over two decades earlier, made the European nations eager to avoid war at any cost. The disillusionment of many Americans with the U.S. involvement in that conflict led the United States to follow an essentially isolationist foreign policy in the following years. In 1938, by the terms of the Munich Pact, France, Great Britain, and Italy surrendered part of Czechoslovakia to Hitler in the hope of appeasing his desire for more territory. The German occupation of Austria went similarly unchecked.

John Kennedy (second from right) and the Choate football team, 1928. Called by one of his teammates a "tiger on the defense," Kennedy, despite a frail constitution, was an undeniably strong athletic competitor.

Kennedy as a member of the Harvard swim team in 1938. His swimming abilities would serve him well during the rescue of his crew from the sunken PT-109 in the Pacific theater of World War II.

During this tense time Jack traveled around Europe and reported his findings to his father; his lifelong interest in history helped him to judge what he saw. He supplemented his senior thesis with the findings of his travels. The paper examined the British policy of appeasement of Nazi Germany and was praised by his instructors for its thoroughness, intelligence, and originality. Jack graduated *cum laude* in the spring of 1940. His father circulated the thesis among his publishing contacts, and after some rewriting by newsman Arthur Krock it was published in July 1940 as *Why England Slept*. The book quickly became a best-seller after its publication. The ambassador was quite proud, even though the book was implicitly critical of Joseph Kennedy's support of the government of Neville Chamberlain, which had been responsible for Britain's Munich policy.

After the German invasion of Poland in September 1939, France and Britain, aware now that appeasement could not work, declared war on Germany. In spring 1940 Winston Churchill replaced Chamberlain as prime minister. Churchill had sounded an early warning about the danger posed by Hitler and had been a vociferous opponent of appeasement. Joseph Kennedy's association with the Chamberlain government and assertions that the United States would not intervene in a war that the Allies (Britain, France, and later the Soviet Union and United States) were destined to lose made him unpopular in both Britain and the United States. In late 1940 the ambassador was recalled to the United States.

By the time the Japanese attacked the American military base at Pearl Harbor, Hawaii, on December 7, 1941, and the United States formally entered World War II, both Joe, Jr., and Jack had already enlisted in the military. Joe, Jr., was accepted as a naval air cadet, but because of Jack's poor health and medical history he was turned down by the army and the navy. After a summer of back-strengthening exercises and some lobbying by his father he was allowed to enlist in the U.S. Navy in September of 1941.

After the navy officers training course Jack was assigned to the Office of Naval Intelligence in Washington, where he prepared bulletins from foreign intelligence reports. When not at work, Jack spent a lot of time with LeMoyne Billings, whom he had first met at Choate and who became a lifelong friend, and with his younger sister Kathleen. In January 1942 Jack was transferred to Charleston, South Carolina. In his new job he instructed defense-plant workers on how to defend themselves and their plants in the event of enemy bombing.

Jack began to find his life as a naval intelligence officer tedious and frustrating. The United States suffered many defeats in the early days of World War II, and like many young men, Jack was anxious to join the fighting. His father contacted some old friends in the government, and at last Jack qualified for sea duty. He transferred to Midshipmen's School

The desire to experience military action during those early post-Pearl Harbor months was hardly exceptional among American men. . . . To duck the challenge of war, to avoid combat . . . simply denied their concept of mission.
—HERBERT S. PARMET historian, on Kennedy's transfer to active duty in the Pacific war, 1942

Joseph Kennedy (center) with his two oldest sons, John (left) and Joseph, Jr., in June 1938, just prior to John's departure for Europe. While there he gathered material for what would become his book *Why England Slept*, a study of Britain's appeasement of Nazi Germany.

at Northwestern University in Evanston, Illinois, in July 1942. When Admiral John Harllee came to the school looking for volunteers for patrol torpedo (PT) boat crews, Jack signed up immediately.

The PT boats were light, maneuverable, and fast and were designed primarily for nighttime use. They had been used to rescue General Douglas Mac-Arthur and his family from the Philippines during the early days of the war in the Pacific. The boats were thought to be especially effective for ship sabotage in the waters around the Southwest Pacific islands. Others thought differently. According to Robert Donovan, author of a 1961 book about Kennedy's time with the PT division, "The truth of it was they probably sank more American tonnage than foreign tonnage."

Jack took command of PT 109 in the spring of 1943, on Tulagi, one of the Solomon Islands, in the South Pacific. On August 1, naval intelligence reported that a convoy of Japanese ships was expected to travel through the area, and 14 PT boats were sent out to intercept the convoy. Early the next morning, after failing to find the Japanese ships, PT 109 was sliced in half by the Japanese destroyer *Amigari* as it was returning to its base. Two of the crew were killed and another three were badly injured. The 11 surviving crew members clung to the hull of the wrecked boat until morning, and when the wreckage began to sink, they were forced to swim three and a half miles to reach Plum Pudding Island. Kennedy towed one of the injured men the entire distance. That night, Kennedy swam back to Ferguson Passage, a route used by PT boats, to try to locate an American ship that could rescue them. Unsuccessful, he returned at dawn. Another swim was tried, with no results. The sailors then swam to another island, closer to the Ferguson Passage. Kennedy again towed the most seriously injured man. Kennedy and another man then swam to still another island, where they discovered two islanders and a canoe. The islanders were sent to Rendova Harbor, nearly 40 miles away, with a message Kennedy had carved into a coconut:

NATIVE KNOWS POSIT [position]/HE CAN PILOT 11 ALIVE/NEED SMALL BOAT/ KENNEDY.

Six days after PT 109 was demolished, Jack Kennedy and his crew were rescued.

Although Kennedy was modest about his actions, the men of his crew were very willing to discuss his courage during the ordeal. Soon he was not only a famous author, but a hero of the war in the Pacific. The story was front-page news in the *New York Times* and the Boston newspapers. Later the noted author John Hersey wrote about the incident in a story for the *New Yorker*, and several books were written about Kennedy's heroism.

Kennedy quickly returned to action at the command of another PT boat. However, the incident had

It was absolutely involuntary. They sank my boat.
—JOHN F. KENNEDY to a high-school student who asked how he became a war hero

aggravated his back problem, and like many other servicemen in the South Pacific, he contracted malaria. Soon thereafter, he was forced to give up his command and return home on medical leave.

On August 12, 1944, Joseph Kennedy, Jr., now serving as a U.S. Navy pilot stationed in England, took off on a secret and highly dangerous bombing mission. Twenty-eight minutes after takeoff, his plane exploded, killing him instantly.

The tragedy shook the entire Kennedy clan. The ambassador mourned the death of his oldest son for the rest of his life. Joe, Jr., had been groomed to fulfill his father's political ambitions. Now Jack would take his place. It was a considerable legacy. As George St. John, the headmaster of Choate Preparatory School, later said: "I'm sure he [Jack] never forgets he must live Joe's life as well as his own."

After spending time in Chelsea Naval Hospital in Boston and then in Arizona and Hollywood, Jack became a reporter for the Hearst newspaper chain, reporting on the founding conference of the United Nations and the election in Britain that removed Winston Churchill as prime minister. Kennedy's byline in the Hearst papers, together with his reputation as a war hero and author, kept his name familiar to the American public, which was helpful for an aspiring politician.

In late April of 1946 Kennedy formally announced his candidacy for the U.S. House of Representatives as Democratic candidate from Massachusetts's 11th congressional district, the old stomping ground of his grandfathers, "Honey Fitz" John Fitzgerald and Patrick Joseph Kennedy. The district was predominantly Irish, working class, and very poor. Kennedy and many of his campaign workers were returning war veterans. Young, often well educated, less likely to be swayed by the religious and secular power of the Catholic church, which was an enormous force in the lives of the Boston Irish, they were a new generation, different from the old-style politicos exemplified by Honey Fitz and the man who had previously held the 11th's seat, James Michael Curley. The campaign did however receive valuable assistance, particularly financial support, from Jo-

I think that if the Kennedy children . . . ever amount to anything, it will be due more to Joe's behavior and his constant example than to any other factor.

—JOHN F. KENNEDY
on the death of his brother,
Joseph, Jr., 1945

seph Kennedy and his old cronies. The rest of the Kennedy family also pitched in. The Kennedy women went door to door and organized tea parties for women voters, brother Robert got himself released from military service to help out, and Honey Fitz campaigned to get out the vote.

Jack Kennedy campaigned tirelessly, despite his bad health. He was a skinny, frail young man whose clothes looked too big and a little shabby, and his speaking style was wooden and stiff. But his interest in the lives and problems of the people was warm and real. His charm and humor came through especially well in question and answer sessions.

The day before the election, Jack marched with the Joseph P. Kennedy, Jr., Brigade of the Veterans of Foreign Wars in a five-mile parade through Boston, but at the parade's end he collapsed and was rushed to a local house. The next day, November 5, 1946, he won the election in a landslide victory, and his political career was launched.

Robert Kennedy is sworn in as a naval aviation cadet in 1943 as his father looks on. Both of Robert's older brothers, Joseph and John, served in the navy during World War II, establishing a Kennedy family tradition.

3

The Young Congressman

Kennedy moved to Washington, D.C., and rented a house in the Georgetown area of the city. In Congress, he was appointed to the Education and Labor Committee, where he served with another freshman congressman, Richard Nixon of California.

While in Congress, Kennedy kept a campaign promise by backing bills that supported housing for veterans. Like his father, he was conservative when it came to economic policy, but he did not agree with Joseph on other issues, most notably foreign policy. Kay Halle, a Washington socialite, remembers an argument between Kennedy and his father at a Washington garden party that ended when Kennedy said, "Now, look here, Dad, you have your political views and I have mine. I'm going to vote exactly the way I feel I must on this."

In 1947 Kennedy went to Europe on a fact-finding tour, stopping first in Ireland to visit his sister Kathleen, who had been married to an English lord and then widowed during the war. After the visit, he went on to London, but before he could continue his trip he was taken ill and rushed to London Clinic. The doctors diagnosed him as suffering from Addison's disease, a malfunction of the adrenal

> *If we're going to change things the way they should be changed, we all have to do things we won't want to do.*
> —JOHN F. KENNEDY

Senator Kennedy with his fiancée, Jacqueline Bouvier, in June 1953. The two met in 1951, when she was working as a photographer at the Washington *Times-Herald*. The bright, cultured, and attractive "Jackie" proved to be the perfect companion for the aspiring politician.

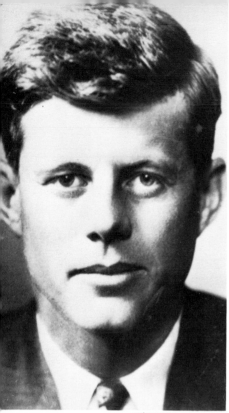

During his early political life Kennedy was plagued by illness and was shaken by the death of his sister Kathleen. Still, he campaigned furiously and was elected to Congress in 1946, 1948, and 1950.

glands that causes weakness, loss of weight, loss of appetite, and reduced immunity to disease. Unchecked infections killed many Addison's patients. He was so sick that a doctor told one of his traveling companions that he would be dead within a year.

The public was told only that Jack had suffered a recurrence of his wartime malaria and that he was planning to sail directly home. Sail home he did, in the hospital cabin of the *Queen Mary*, but this, too, was kept from the public. His father knew that such a grave illness would destroy any chances Kennedy had for higher public office, but Kennedy himself was ferociously competitive and always resisted any suggestions that his poor health made him any less capable of keeping up with others. During his first term in Congress, he attended a football game with his friends Torbert and Phyllis MacDonald. As he pulled himself painfully up the stairs to the grandstand, Phyllis said to her husband, "For God's sake grab his elbow and help him." Torby MacDonald, a friend from Jack's Harvard days, said, "No! Don't even mention it!"

Kennedy's disease was controlled by a new cortisone drug called DOCA (desoxycorticosterone acetate), which, in pellet form, was implanted under the skin in his thighs. He made sure that emergency supplies were stashed in safe-deposit boxes around the country.

Despite his ill health, Kennedy rapidly acquired a reputation as a playboy. He dated a great many women but never had a serious, long-term relationship with any of them. At the time, Kennedy believed that he would only live for a few more years. Marriage seemed out of the question.

On May 12, 1948, while his sister Kathleen and her friend Lord Peter Fitzwilliam were flying in France, their tiny plane crashed into a mountain. They were both killed. Of all the Kennedy children, Joe, Jr., and Kathleen were the ones closest to Jack; now both were dead, and he expected that he, too, would die within a few years. He went through a period of great depression, talking to his friends about death. He told George Smathers that "The point is that you've got to live every day like it's your last day on earth. That's what I'm doing." Eventually his depression subsided, but it left him with an urge to do his best, to live each moment fully, to burn more brightly than anyone else in the little time he thought he had.

Jack was reelected to Congress in 1948 and 1950, but he was bored by the House of Representatives, about which he said, "We're just worms. Nobody pays much attention to us nationally." As a junior congressman, he was mostly involved with domestic issues, while his real interest was in foreign affairs. He decided to run for the Senate. In early 1951, he went on another trip to Europe, touring West Germany, Spain, Yugoslavia, and installations of the newly formed North Atlantic Treaty Organization (NATO). After his return, he made a radio report in which he gave his views of the European situation. While he agreed with the view that Western Europe should be a first line of defense against possible Soviet aggression, he felt that the allied countries of NATO should share the burden of rearmament. It was also his feeling that the Soviet Union was unlikely to risk a confrontation in Europe. In October of 1951 he began a trip from Israel to the Far East. He took his sister Pat and his brother Robert with him.

Because of the difference in their ages (John was eight years older), Kennedy had never paid much attention to Robert before, but during the course of this trip he discovered Robert's toughness, intensity, and loyalty. It was the beginning of a very close relationship that would last the rest of Kennedy's brief life.

Jack was deeply influenced by his Far Eastern trip, particularly by what he saw in Vietnam. Vietnam was then under French rule, and the French had been involved in a long, fruitless war against communist and nationalist rebels there. The ruling classes in the capital, Saigon, lived off the money brought in by French foreign aid, ignoring the welfare of the peasants in the countryside. Jack decided that if communism was to be stopped, the United States would have to provide something more than economic and military aid. The people of developing

At least half of the days that he spent on this earth were days of intense physical pain. . . . But during all this time, I never heard him complain. I never heard him say anything that would indicate that he felt God had dealt with him unjustly.
—ROBERT F. KENNEDY
on his brother's illnesses

countries would have to see that democracy, not communism, was the real step forward and was consistent with their growing nationalism. He also foresaw the eventual end of colonial rule in Asia.

In Japan, Jack became sick again. When he returned to the United States he had recovered enough to make another radio report, in which he talked about the ideas he had developed during the trip and his beliefs about America's role in helping the poorer countries of the world.

On April 6, 1952, Jack began his campaign for the Senate against Senator Henry Cabot Lodge, a Republican. Lodge came from a distinguished Massachusetts family (his grandfather and namesake had defeated "Honey Fitz" Fitzgerald for the Senate in 1916) and had great influence in the state; Kennedy had a much less substantial reputation. In response the Kennedy family put together what

John Kennedy with his brothers Edward (left) and Robert. Eight years younger than John, Robert was never close to his brother while the two were boys. It was not until the early 1950s that the two became constant, loyal companions.

came to be called the "Kennedy machine," an expertly run organization of loyal and hardworking people, including many who would be closely associated with Kennedy in future years: Lawrence O'Brien, Kenneth O'Donnell, David Powers, and, of course, Robert Kennedy.

Joseph Kennedy was determined to run the campaign. To him Lodge and his family connections epitomized the Massachusetts establishment from which Joseph, as an Irishman and Catholic, had been excluded. But politics had changed since World War II, and Joseph's often overbearing style alienated many of Kennedy's young staffers. O'Donnell persuaded Kennedy that someone was needed to talk to and rein in his father; it was at this point that Robert was persuaded to leave his job at the Justice Department and help run his older brother's campaign. Nevertheless, Joseph's energy, expertise, and financial resources were invaluable.

Unlike the rest of the family, Robert was not comfortable speaking in public and for the most part remained behind the scenes. His first public speech lasted less than 25 seconds: "My brother Jack couldn't be here. My mother couldn't be here. My sister Eunice couldn't be here. My sister Pat couldn't be here. My sister Jean couldn't be here. But if my brother Jack were here, he'd tell you Lodge has a very bad voting record. Thank you." He gained a reputation for being aggressive and ruthless, with something of a mean streak, but Kennedy appreciated his work and loyalty. In a heated moment during the campaign, he told one of his workers: "He's the only one who doesn't stick knives in my back, the only one I can count on when it comes down to it." Kennedy never changed his opinion of Robert.

Although most political observers believed that Lodge would beat Kennedy, Jack got 51 percent of the vote, enough of a margin to take Lodge's seat in the Senate. Despite the overwhelming Republican majority in the presidential election, in which Dwight Eisenhower defeated Adlai Stevenson, the young Democratic challenger had defeated the incumbent Republican.

> *I told him Joe was dead and it was his responsibility to run for Congress. He didn't want it. But I told him he had to.*
> —JOSEPH P. KENNEDY, Sr. on Jack's decision to run for Congress in 1946

John and Jacqueline Kennedy leave Saint Mary's Church, Newport, Rhode Island, following their wedding on September 12, 1953. The popular senator and his wife were greeted by more than 1,000 people outside the church, and the wedding was covered by the media as one of the major social events of the year.

The Senate offered Kennedy a greater opportunity to work on foreign affairs. Drawing on his experiences in Indochina, as the Asian peninsula containing Vietnam, Cambodia, Laos, and other countries was known, he opposed the Eisenhower administration's request for $400 million in military assistance for France, insisting that money should also be spent for nonmilitary aid for Vietnam. In a speech before the Senate on April 6, he said: "To pour money, material and men into the jungles of Indochina without at least a remote prospect of victory would be dangerously futile and self-destructive. . . . I am frankly of the belief that no amount of American military assistance in Indochina can conquer an enemy that is everywhere and at the same time nowhere." He was referring to the guerrilla warfare conducted by the Viet Minh, the communist-backed, anticolonial rebels in North Vietnam. He believed that a communist takeover in Vietnam would be likely to lead to the same sort of takeover in the rest of Asia, a school of thought sometimes referred to as the "domino theory." Kennedy believed that rather than supporting France's attempt at a military solution, which was likely to be ultimately unsuccessful, the United States could enlist the support of the Vietnamese people — many of whom, out of nationalism, supported the efforts of the Viet Minh to overthrow French colonial rule — and avoid a communist victory by working toward establishing self-rule and political, economic, and social reforms.

Kennedy also criticized the administration for talking tough about retaliation against Soviet aggression and expansionism while moving to cut the defense budget, arguing that heedlessly economizing on defense would compromise national security and weaken the effectiveness of U.S. foreign policy. Kennedy's foreign affairs views did not please his father, and the two men simply stopped discussing them.

In 1951 Kennedy had been introduced to Jacqueline Bouvier. She came from a wealthy, upperclass background and ran in the same Washington social circle as Kennedy. When he met her, she was the inquiring photographer at the *Washington Times-Herald*, a position once held by his sister Kathleen. Known as Jackie, she was cultured, well dressed, and combined intelligence and beauty in a way that fascinated Kennedy.

Though Jackie was equally attracted to him, she found the Kennedy family hard to deal with. Their teasing and rough sports were foreign to her, and after she broke her ankle playing touch football, she refused to participate in any of their sports. However, she and Joseph Kennedy grew quite fond of each other.

Kennedy's courtship of Jackie continued until the spring of 1953, when he proposed by telegram while she was on assignment in Paris. Their wedding on September 12, 1953, was one of the social events of the year. Afterwards, the new Mrs. Kennedy set about domesticating her husband. One of Kennedy's congressional colleagues had said that he looked like a college freshman, referring not only to Kennedy's thinness and his youthful face but to his sloppy style of dressing. Under his wife's tutelage Kennedy paid more attention to his clothes and tried to share her appreciation of the arts.

He was never really interested in local politics or in the city of Boston. He was always interested in the U.S. as part of the world.
—HIRSH FREED
journalist, on Kennedy's interest in foreign policy

4

The Race for the Presidency

The Soviet Union, to that point the world's only communist state, and the United States emerged from World War II as the strongest nations of the world. The mutual distrust and global rivalry for power that developed between the two wartime allies has been termed the cold war. In the United States the early cold war years were characterized by suspicion and fear of domestic communist subversion, intensified by the discovery by the House of Representatives Un-American Activities Committee (HUAC) of communists within the government and the establishment of communist regimes in China and Eastern Europe. Anticommunism became the key political issue of the day; the spectacular early career of Kennedy's congressional counterpart Richard Nixon was due in large part to his HUAC activities and reputation as an anticommunist.

As the fear of communism continued to grow in the early 1950s, Senator Joseph McCarthy of Wisconsin took redbaiting to another level. (Communists were often referred to as "Reds.") Seizing on anticommunism as a sure way to political prominence, he made irresponsible and undocumented

It's a gift. He doesn't know how to be stuffy.
—ARTHUR KROCK
journalist, on
Kennedy's charm

Kennedy greets a crowd in Denver, Colorado, during his 1960 presidential campaign. As the Eisenhower years faded into history, Kennedy emerged as a symbol of America's future. For many, Kennedy — young, confident, forward-looking — was the man to lead the country into a new era.

Accompanied by Jacqueline, Kennedy hobbles into a New York hospital on October 10, 1954, to undergo back surgery. He suffered intense back pain throughout most of his life.

charges. Those accused, falsely or not, of being communists or even of having past associations with communists often had their lives and careers damaged. McCarthy's tactics ultimately became as great an issue as communism. "McCarthyism" posed a special problem for Kennedy. Kennedy and McCarthy had been freshmen representatives together and traveled in the same social circles. McCarthy was a frequent guest at Kennedy's Georgetown house and the Kennedy family compound at Hyannis Port (on Cape Cod in Massachusetts) and sometimes dated Kennedy's sister Patricia. Joseph Kennedy was an especially vocal supporter of McCarthy and his claims of communist infiltration in the government. As a young politician Kennedy also had taken a strong stand against communism, especially as a member of the House

Education and Labor Committee. Though unquestionably prolabor, Kennedy managed to extract damaging testimony about communist influence in unions from labor representatives called before the committee. He, like other politicians, was praised for his tough stance.

In March 1954 McCarthy grew too reckless when he accused the Protestant clergy and the U.S. Army of widespread communism. Eisenhower, wary of McCarthy from the start, rejected the senator's requests for access to F.B.I. files and denounced him publicly.

In September and October of 1954 the Senate was prepared to vote on an official censure (a vote of disapproval) of McCarthy. Kennedy was in a difficult position. While he did not support McCarthy's crusade, he also would not criticize him publicly. Joseph Kennedy's support for McCarthy was unabated, and a Kennedy vote for censure was certain to displease and embarrass his father. Kennedy's health had continued to be a problem, and it was to solve the problem for him.

By mid-1954 his back was giving him so much pain that he had trouble walking even with the help of crutches. It was thought that an operation to fuse some of the disks in his back might help, but his Addison's disease made such an operation very hazardous. He was in so much pain, though, that he convinced the doctors to take the chance, and on October 10, 1954, he was admitted to the hospital. The doctors were right to be concerned; after the operation on October 21, Kennedy contracted a staph infection and lapsed into a coma. It was thought that he would die. Eventually he began to recover, although he did not leave the hospital until just before Christmas. While he was recuperating, the Senate recommended that McCarthy be "condemned" rather than "censured." On December 2 the Senate condemned McCarthy by a vote of 67-22, effectively ending his influence. Kennedy was not present.

His convalescence was long and difficult and included a second operation on his back. At about the same time a new doctor recommended he change his Addison's medication from the DOCA pellets to an oral form of cortisone. The change greatly improved his stamina and overall health and added weight to his slender frame.

While he recovered, Kennedy and his staff began the research and writing that became his book *Profiles in Courage*, which won the Pulitzer Prize in 1957. The book portrayed senators throughout American history who had maintained their personal integrity by taking courageous and often unpopular stands.

To this point, Kennedy had enjoyed a stellar career and was judged a rising star in national politics. His books had brought him before the public eye, as had his actions in the Senate. He had a beautiful wife who was expecting a child. He was surrounded by a loyal and talented staff, could call upon the support of a wealthy and well-connected father, and had a crack political organization at his disposal for election campaigns. In 1956 he attended the Democratic National Convention as a supporter of Adlai Stevenson, who once again would oppose Eisen-

Kennedy nominates Adlai Stevenson for president at the Democratic National Convention in 1956. Stevenson, a former governor of Illinois, considered choosing Kennedy as his running mate but instead selected Estes Kefauver, dealing Kennedy the first political defeat of his career.

hower in the national election. Stevenson, formerly governor of Illinois, was considering three Democratic senators for the vice-presidency: Estes Kefauver from Tennessee, Hubert Humphrey from Minnesota, and John Kennedy from Massachusetts. All could rally significant support for the Democrats in their areas of the country, a necessary thing for a presidential candidate seeking nationwide appeal, but the three hopefuls also had blocks of loyal support within the Democratic party. Not wishing to damage party unity by his choice, Stevenson shifted the burden of responsibility to the convention delegates. They would nominate the vice-presidential candidate. It appeared possible that Kennedy, whose nominating speech for Stevenson had been very well received by the delegates, would be the first Catholic nominated for high public office in the United States since Alfred E. Smith had been nominated as the Democratic presidential candidate in 1928. However, after three ballots Estes Kefauver became Stevenson's running mate. Sorely disappointed with his defeat, Kennedy left Jackie with her family in Newport, Rhode Island, and flew to Europe for a brief vacation. While he was gone, Jackie had a miscarriage. Kennedy cut short his trip and flew back immediately.

Nevertheless, 1956 had been an important year for John Kennedy. Although he had suffered his first political defeat at the Democratic convention, his performance there had further enhanced his popularity with the public. He was coming into his own, beginning to move out from under his father's influence, achieving prominence as a true national political figure. Although his deceased older brother, Joseph, Jr., still cast a long shadow, Kennedy was able to put that legacy (and his own failure) in perspective. After Stevenson's lopsided defeat by Eisenhower in 1956, Kennedy said: "Joe would have won the nomination [for the vice-presidency], and then he and Stevenson would have been beaten by Eisenhower and today Joe's political career would be in shambles and he would be trying to pick up the pieces." His own career, in contrast, remained intact.

> *The true democracy, living and growing and inspiring, puts faith in the people — faith that the people will not simply elect men who will represent their views ably and faithfully, but also elect men who will exercise their conscientious judgment — faith that the people will not condemn those whose devotion to principle leads them to unpopular causes, but will reward courage, respect honor and ultimately recognize right.*
> —JOHN F. KENNEDY
> from *Profiles in Courage* (1956)

Unbloodied by the Democratic defeat in 1956, Kennedy took advantage of his high profile by making more than 300 speeches nationwide during the next two years. His campaign for reelection to the Senate in 1958 brought him a smashing victory, as he earned 73.6 percent of a record turnout. His win brought even further publicity, and he was mentioned almost immediately afterward as a front-runner for the Democratic presidential nomination in 1960. Plans for his campaign began shortly thereafter, and he officially announced his candidacy for the nomination on January 2, 1960.

Both his political views and his religion were major issues in Kennedy's campaign for the nomination. Kennedy favored policies that supported the United States while working against the influence of the Soviet Union. The Democrats worried that he was not liberal enough, that his concern for foreign affairs would alienate those who had come to expect FDR-style domestic spending from the Democrats. The more explosive potential issue was his religion.

During the early centuries after the discovery of America, most European countries had an official state religion, and people who followed beliefs other than the official state religion were persecuted. Many of America's first settlers left Europe for this reason. The U.S. Constitution contains a provision for separation between church (religion) and state in the United States. In this way, people are free to practice their own religions, and the government cannot impose any one set of religious beliefs upon the citizens or persecute people who do not follow a particular religion.

Since a tenet of the Catholic faith holds the pope, the head of the Roman Catholic religion, to be infallible when speaking on faith and morals, many Americans were worried that a Catholic president would feel his primary responsibility to be to the pope rather than the American people and the Constitution should a conflict arise. The issue came up many times during the campaign: At one point Kennedy silenced his critics by saying: "If a President breaks his oath he is not only committing a crime against the Constitution, for which the Congress

Jack was indeed a playboy in public office until 1958. . . . It [the run for the presidency] meant a complete redesigning of his public image.
—WILLIAM O. DOUGLAS
Supreme Court justice, on the 1960 campaign

can impeach and should impeach him, but he is committing a sin against his God." This and other similar statements assured voters that Kennedy would act according to the dictates of his own conscience, independent of the Catholic hierarchy. Catholicism was a target of prejudice from many Americans who associated it with the immigrant groups who had come to the country, but Kennedy appealed to the higher instincts of the electorate. "If this election is decided on the basis that 40 million Americans lost their chance of being president on the day they were baptized," he said, "then it is the whole nation that will be the loser in the eyes of history, and in the eyes of our own people." Kennedy was largely able to defuse Catholicism as an issue in the campaign.

Kennedy won the Democratic nomination in July and chose Senator Lyndon Baines Johnson of Texas as his vice-presidential running mate. Johnson had served as the Senate majority leader and wielded great power in Congress. He could also help bring in the Southern vote for the Democrats.

During the presidential campaign, Kennedy met his opponent, Richard M. Nixon, in a series of televised debates. The first was the most decisive. Nixon, who had made an issue of Kennedy's youth and relative inexperience, seemed unprepared and uncomfortable in comparison with the polished, handsome Kennedy.

Kennedy, in hard hat and goggles, visits a U.S. Steel plant in Gary, Indiana, during the 1960 presidential campaign. Like his father, Kennedy was prolabor and was a favorite among working-class people across the country.

The Republicans nominated Richard Nixon, who had been Eisenhower's vice-president. Eisenhower was a popular president, and Nixon started well ahead of Kennedy in the polls.

Despite Eisenhower's popularity, many Americans felt that the country's competitive edge had been dulled after World War II, especially after the Soviet Union launched the first space satellite, *Sputnik.* There was concern that America was losing its postwar superiority in science, technology, and influence in world affairs; many people also felt that the Eisenhower years were gray ones, without excitement or a sense of national purpose.

Kennedy promised to change that, to "get the country moving again." During four television debates with Nixon he came across as cool and in command, and he made it clear that he believed America had to move forward aggressively if it was to keep its place in the world. Kennedy's campaign seemed to promise excitement and challenge ("challenge" was one of his favorite words), and the country seemed ready for it. He defeated Nixon in November of 1960 by a slim margin.

In the days between the election and his inauguration in late January of 1961, Kennedy met with Eisenhower and formed panels of advisers to help him during his administration. There were 79 in all, employing nearly 100 people. He wanted a broad and deep pool of information and studies on which to base his presidential decisions. When questioned about it he replied, "I simply cannot afford to have just one set of advisers." He also regarded the task forces as testing grounds for future government appointments.

His talent hunt resulted in some surprising choices for key positions within the administration, but Kennedy was determined to surround himself with "the best and the brightest" people he could find. Robert McNamara, Kennedy's choice to head the Defense Department, was a Republican who had previously been president of the Ford Motor Company. As secretary of the treasury, Kennedy tabbed Douglas Dillon, a prominent Republican who had held the same position in the Eisenhower administration. The secretary of state was comparatively little-known Dean Rusk (Stevenson was viewed as a leading candidate), while McGeorge Bundy, a young — 41 — Harvard professor and yet another Republican, was chosen to be one of Kennedy's top foreign policy advisers. His selection of his brother Robert as attorney general drew much criticism, as Robert had never practiced as an attorney or tried a case.

> *The torch has been passed to a new generation of Americans — born in this century, tempered by war, disciplined by a hard and bitter peace, proud of our ancient heritage.*
> —JOHN F. KENNEDY
> inaugural address

UPI/BETTMANN NEWSPHOTOS

The Democratic presidential nominee and his wife are welcomed to New York City by a ticker tape parade on October 19, 1960. Kennedy selected Senate majority leader Lyndon Johnson as his running mate primarily for his influence in Congress and his popularity in the South.

UPI/BETTMANN NEWSPHOTOS

Kennedy gives his inaugural address on January 21, 1961, in Washington, D.C. Chief Justice Earl Warren is seated at left; Vice-president Johnson is at right. In his speech Kennedy issued a challenge to Americans to work together to solve the country's problems.

Jacqueline had given birth to their second child and first son, John Fitzgerald Kennedy, Jr., just after Thanksgiving in 1960. Their daughter, Caroline, had been born in 1957; for the first time in decades, there would be young children in the White House. It seemed that the Kennedys were bringing youth, enthusiasm, and change to America.

Inauguration Day — January 21, 1961 — was cold and snowy in Washington, D.C., but the weather did not cool the excitement that Kennedy brought with him to the office of president. His speech was one of the shortest ever given by a newly inaugurated president: he said that a new generation of Americans had taken over, and he offered the coun-

try not easy solutions and a lack of change, but the challenge of hard work: "Let every nation know . . . that we shall pay any price, bear any burden, meet any hardship, support any friend, oppose any foe, to assure the survival and the success of liberty. . . . Let us never negotiate out of fear. But let us never fear to negotiate. . . . All this will not be finished in the first one hundred days. Nor will it be finished in the first one thousand days, nor in the life of this Administration, nor even perhaps in our lifetime on this planet. But let us begin." He finished with a ringing call to the country: "And so, my fellow Americans: ask not what your country can do for you — ask what you can do for your country."

5

The New Frontier

From the beginning, the Kennedy administration brought great changes to the White House and to Washington. In direct contrast to the military formality of Eisenhower, Kennedy had little patience with the formal ceremonies White House protocol demanded, and his staff often felt like family members in a home. Formal lines of authority and delegations of responsibility meant little to the president; he was concerned with results. One biographer noted that "Assignments sometimes landed on the fellow who happened to be in the Oval Office [with the president] at the particular moment of need." Instead of letting his secretaries contact people for him, Kennedy would often dial calls himself, which surprised a number of staffers who picked up their phones only to discover the president on the line.

He liked question and answer sessions with his staff and advisers, and he read everything he could get his hands on, from the major newspapers and magazines to the many memos and studies prepared for him. Carl Kaysen, National Security deputy for military and strategic matters, said: "There wasn't anybody there who had not had some personal contact with Kennedy from time to time."

The New Frontier of which I speak is not a set of promises — it is a set of challenges. It sums up not what I intend to offer the American people, but what I intend to ask of them.
—JOHN F. KENNEDY
nomination acceptance
speech, July 1960

The first family poses for an informal portrait on Easter Sunday, 1963, in Palm Beach, Florida. The children are John, Jr., age two, and Caroline, age five.

UPI/BETTMANN NEWSPHOTOS

UPI/BETTMANN NEWSPHOTOS

Kennedy went before Congress on January 30, 1961, to deliver his first state of the union address. Stressing the difficult challenges that the United States faced, he outlined the means by which he intended to lead the country into "the new frontier" but warned that "life in 1961 [would] not be easy."

Jacqueline, too, made a major impact on the White House, as she began to restore the building to its original grandeur and historical importance. She organized a White House Fine Arts Committee, had the mansion declared a national monument by Congress, and arranged for the 1962 publication of the *White House Guide Book*. Jacqueline had been responsible for introducing her husband to the world of fine art and classical music, and now she extended that introduction to the rest of the nation, bringing artists, Nobel Prize winners, and gifted musicians to the White House. It seemed that the new administration had more than a touch of class, leading eventually to the perception of the Kennedy administration as a sort of Camelot, populated by bright, eager young idealists willing and able to change the world for the better.

During his early days in office, it seemed that John Kennedy could do no wrong. He helped foster the impression himself, exuding confidence and vigor in the ten press conferences he gave in the first three months. The nation's economy gradually improved, and many of his first actions were designed to correct problems at home and abroad.

Adolf Berle, a member of the Latin American Task Force, wrote in his diary that Kennedy "has had more rough crises thrown at him in the first sixty days of his administration than any President since Lincoln." In addition to poverty and discrimination in the United States, Kennedy faced the threat of Soviet-sponsored communism in Latin America (particularly in Cuba), an accelerating nuclear arms race with the Soviet Union, civil wars and American promises of assistance in Southeast Asia, unrest in Africa, and the cold war that existed between the United States and the Soviet Union and China.

On January 30, 1961, John Kennedy delivered his first state of the union address to Congress, outlining these problems and his proposals for solving them. He said, "Life in 1961 will not be easy. . . . There will be further setbacks before the tide is turned. But turn it we must. The hopes of all mankind rest upon us."

During his election campaign Kennedy had traveled through West Virginia and been shocked by the poverty he saw there. His first executive order as president was to double the ration of surplus government food given to 4 million poor people.

There had never been such youthful euphoria in Washington since the early days of the New Deal.
—SAMUEL ELIOT MORISON
historian

Kennedy believed that the United States not only needed to give military help to underdeveloped countries but also food, education, and medical assistance. During his state of the union address, he announced the formation of the Food for Peace Program, in which surplus American food was sent to needy countries abroad. In March his executive order created the Peace Corps, to be headed by his brother-in-law Robert Sargent Shriver.

The Peace Corps consisted of Americans willing to go abroad to put their skills and education to work for the people of developing nations. The Peace Corps was not a foreign aid package; the idea was

A Peace Corps volunteer works with a group of native Africans. Kennedy established the Peace Corps in March 1961, envisioning the group as an organization that would provide education to citizens of underdeveloped nations to enable them to develop their own long-range solutions to economic and social problems.

(and is) for American volunteers to teach the people of third world countries to help themselves develop their own long-range solutions to problems. The idea caught the imagination of America's youth, and 5,000 young Americans quickly volunteered to join the Peace Corps. They would work in 47 countries during the Kennedy administration, building health centers, schools and bridges; teaching farming and agriculture. Living under the same conditions as the people they were sent to help, the volunteers did much to foster an image of the United States as a nation willing to aid progress in the poorer nations of the world.

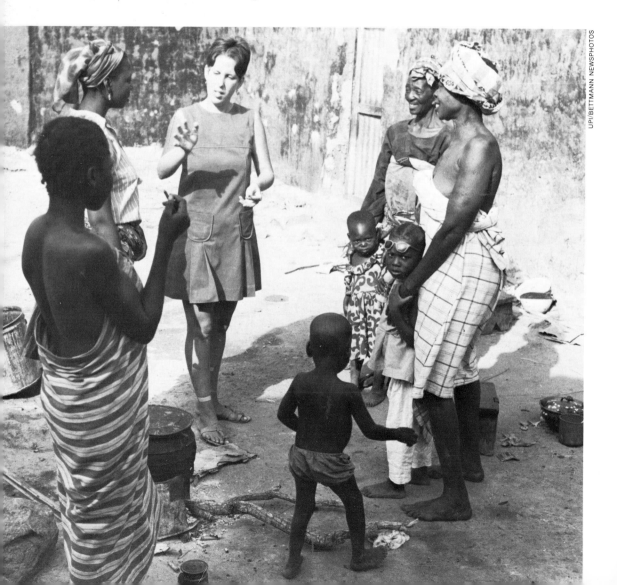

The Alliance for Progress was a much more overtly political program. Aimed at Latin America, long noted for its turbulent politics and repressive dictatorships, its goal was to "immunize" the area against revolutionary, specifically communist, movements through foreign aid aimed at promoting long-term economic development and social reform. The hope was that by making peaceful change possible, the Alliance for Progress would eliminate the need for violent upheaval. The program was criticized by many as idealistic and was not particularly successful. Latin American politics continued to be characterized by instability and repression.

Kennedy's early presidency was also marked by increased tension in Southeast Asia. Although the United States was concerned with the situation in Vietnam, Kennedy's immediate concern was with Laos, a landlocked country bordered by the communist nations of China and North Vietnam to the north, and by South Vietnam, Cambodia, and Thailand to the south.

North Vietnamese president Ho Chi Minh (left) visits Poland in 1957. Ho led the Viet Minh in their successful efforts to overthrow French colonial rule in Vietnam. During the 1960s, he led the North Vietnamese and Viet Cong struggle to establish a communist government over a united Vietnam.

Between 1949 and 1951, in the face of a growing independence movement, the Laotian royal family struggled to retain the constitutional monarchy granted to them by France. One prince, Souphanouvong, joined the communist leader Ho Chi Minh in Vietnam and formed the Pathet Lao ("Land of the Lao") to free his country of French imperialist forces. His half brother Souvanna Phouma led the regular government in Vientiane, the capital of Laos. The Pathet Lao invaded and occupied two provinces in the northeast in 1953. An agreement made in Geneva the following year called for a cease-fire and sanctioned the establishment of the Pathet Lao in northern Laos. The western nations saw Laos and its coalition government as a buffer between China and North Vietnam and the noncommunist countries of Cambodia and South Vietnam.

Kennedy and British prime minister Harold Macmillan (far right) conferred on March 26, 1961, in an effort to achieve a cease-fire in the civil war in Laos. Though a cease-fire was achieved in May of that year, it was short-lived.

As the French prepared to withdraw from Vietnam, Cambodia, and Laos in 1954, the United States entered into an agreement designed to protect the peninsula from communism. This agreement, called the Southeast Asia Treaty Organization (SEATO), also included Thailand, Pakistan, the Philippines, Great Britain, France, Australia, and New Zealand. Under the SEATO plan, Laos, with U.S. economic aid, was to develop a large army to fight communism. By the end of 1960 the United States had poured $300 million into the country, almost all for military purposes. The Royal Laotian Army was outfitted and trained in conventional military maneuvers, not in the type of guerrilla warfare that communist forces favored in Southeast Asia. Instead of improving the standard of living or even producing a good army, the American aid produced

UPI/BETTMANN NEWSPHOTOS

greed, bribery, waste, and corruption. The peasants in the countryside did not benefit from the money, which made the communist promises of a better life seem very bright. The Central Intelligence Agency (CIA) intervened in the government, which did nothing to ease the Laotians' mistrust of the United States.

By the time of Kennedy's inauguration, the coalition government had collapsed, and another civil war was in progress in Laos. Willing to test the resolve of the new president, the Soviet Union had increased its airlifts of military materials to the Pathet Lao in the north. Kennedy hoped for a peaceful government in Laos that did not depend on either communist or American backing, but events seemed to be making this less likely to occur. Eventually he realized that the United States had to make the Soviet Union understand that the choice was between a neutral Laos or a Laos bolstered with direct American military intervention.

Kennedy therefore ordered American troops in the Pacific to move toward Southeast Asia and received pledges of help from India and most of the SEATO countries. The Soviet Union agreed to begin negotiations toward peace in Laos and a cease-fire was arranged in May 1961. Although Kennedy judged his actions a success, the Laotian problem was just the starting point for ever-increasing U.S. involvement in Southeast Asia. The unstable government established in Laos after the cease-fire and U.S. reassurances to South Vietnam and Thailand that we would not abandon them to communism led to secret and then open involvement in the Vietnam War.

At the same time Kennedy was directing U.S. efforts in Laos, he was also concerned with events closer to home. On the Caribbean island of Cuba, just 90 miles from the American mainland, Fidel Castro, after courting both the United States and the Soviet Union, had moved his country clearly into the Soviet camp, becoming the only communist nation of Latin America. Castro had led the 1958 revolution that overthrew dictator Fulgencio Batista and was so popular that, as the last ambassador to Cuba noted, "The same masses who in 1959 roared

We had to stay in Vietnam until we left on terms other than a retreat or abandonment of our commitment.
—THEODORE SORENSEN
Kennedy aide, on
the administration's
Vietnam policy

their approval of his democratic and then of his humanistic pronouncements shouted themselves hoarse approving his Marxism in 1961." Cuba's proximity and the fear that Castro's communist revolution might spread through the rest of Latin America greatly alarmed the United States. Just before Kennedy's inauguration, the Eisenhower administration had severed diplomatic ties with Cuba; plans were made to use a small group of exiled Cubans, known as the Cuban Brigade, to invade the island and overthrow Castro. It was thought that Cubans dissatisfied with the Castro regime would rally to the invaders. The entire operation was to appear to be the work of Cuban exiles without direct ties to Washington.

Kennedy stands before a map of Southeast Asia during a press conference in March 1961. Kennedy's assurances to the governments of the region that the United States would not abandon them to communist aggression set the stage for the long and bitter history of U.S. military involvement in that area.

61

Despite his skepticism about the invasion plans made by the preceding administration, Kennedy approved the Cuban invasion. Publicly he promised that the United States had no intention of moving against Cuba, but privately he met with his advisers, the military, and the CIA in order to oversee the operation.

On Sunday, April 17, 1961, while the Cuban Brigade began its invasion of Cuba, Kennedy attended morning mass. He spent the afternoon watching steeplechase races with Jacqueline and playing golf with his brother-in-law Steve Smith. He discussed the Cuban invasion with Smith and said to him, "It just doesn't feel right."

The president's instinct was correct. By Monday morning the invasion was a disaster. The CIA had recruited 1,400 Cuban exiles in Miami and sent them to Guatemala for training and had purchased

Cuban leader Fidel Castro delivers a television address in Havana in 1960. Castro's revolution of 1958, which ousted Fulgencio Batista, established the first communist government in the western hemisphere.

some World War II B-26 bomber planes and six old freighter ships; the recruitment, training, and purchases were to appear as something that the Cubans had done themselves. The plan called for the brigade to land on two beaches (code-named Red Beach and Blue Beach) on the Bay of Pigs, on Cuba's southern shore. A U.S. destroyer was supposed to lead the freighters to the island, a U.S. aircraft carrier was to wait in the area, and U.S. jets were supposed to fly reconnaissance missions to assess the Cubans' military strengths and weaknesses.

Red Beach was protected by coral reefs, but the CIA either did not know about them or did not tell the brigade about them. Many of the landing craft were ripped open by the reefs. Blue Beach was surrounded by swamps. Although the brigade had been told that their invasion would be supported by U.S. air strikes, at the last minute Kennedy canceled the air raids. Despite the president's orders, the first man on the beach was an American. The Cuban response was personally directed by Castro, who knew the area well—it was his favorite fishing spot.

Although it had originally been thought that the invaders could hide in the mountains and direct a popular Cuban uprising against Castro, the Bay of Pigs was too far from the mountains to make such a plan feasible. The popular support within Cuba that the invaders had counted on had not materialized. Senator Claiborne Pell had visited Cuba in the spring of 1961 and reported that he did not think the people of Cuba would revolt against Castro because most of Castro's enemies were either in jail, dead, or had left the country. Pell's report seemed not to have reached the president, but it was certainly true that the Cuban people showed no signs of rising up against Fidel Castro.

The men of the Cuban Brigade were quickly pinned down in the swamps surrounding the Bay of Pigs, unable to move forward or backward. As Castro's forces closed in on them, they ran short of ammunition. Cuban planes bombed and strafed the brigade's vessels, destroying one that held almost all of the communications equipment.

> *All my life I've known better than to depend on the experts. How could I have been so stupid, to let them go ahead?*
> —JOHN F. KENNEDY
> on the Bay of Pigs

Having received news of the disaster, Kennedy and his advisers met almost around the clock. Some advisers called for immediate U.S. air strikes, but Kennedy still hoped to hide the U.S. involvement and refused to approve. He also refused to allow a destroyer to help the brigade, but he finally agreed on Tuesday to allow six unmarked jet fighters to act as cover for a B-26 bomber attack from Nicaragua. The jets encountered heavy fire over Cuba, and four U.S. airmen were killed.

Of the nearly 1,400 members of the Cuban Brigade, only 150 were evacuated. The rest were captured or killed. The operation was a complete disaster, and the extent of U.S. involvement was soon made public. Protest demonstrations took place from Latin America to New York and San Francisco. In Washington, it seemed that everyone was busy trying to redirect the blame. On April 19 Fidel Castro broadcast a stinging condemnation of the United States, but on the same day John Kennedy told a news conference: "There's an old saying that victory has a hundred fathers and defeat is an orphan." He took total responsibility for the fiasco.

Anti-Castro demonstrators make their anger known in New York City on April 27, 1961, ten days after the failed Bay of Pigs invasion. Kennedy's attempt to oust Castro was perhaps his administration's greatest foreign policy blunder.

The next day the White House officially repeated the statement: "President Kennedy has stated from the beginning that as President he bears sole responsibility. . . . The President is strongly opposed to anyone within or without the administration attempting to shift the responsibility."

Kennedy, taking action as always, asked some of his trusted advisers to try to pin down what exactly had gone wrong, but the bright excitement of his early days in office had been tarnished. Charles Spalding, an old friend of Kennedy's, said: "After that he was totally different in his attitude toward everything. . . . Before the Bay of Pigs, everything was a glorious adventure, onward and upward. Afterwards it was a series of ups and downs, with terrible pitfalls, suspicion everywhere, cautious of everything, questioning always."

More than anything else, the Bay of Pigs failure served to settle John Kennedy into his job, to help him understand the limits of U.S. power, the potential for disaster that existed when that power was misused, and the seriousness of the challenges he would have to face every day that he was in office.

A group gathers in front of a store window display to watch Kennedy deliver a televised message in July 1961. The Bay of Pigs fiasco had a sobering effect on the president, revealing to him the limits of U.S. power. Surprisingly, his popularity in the public opinion polls increased immediately after the invasion.

6
Berlin and the Soviet Union

In 1957 the Soviet Union had amazed the world by launching *Sputnik*, the first space satellite. In April 1961, the Soviet Union announced that Yuri Gagarin, a Soviet cosmonaut (astronaut), had made the first manned orbital flight around the earth.

America's space program had begun just after World War II, but it had always suffered from lack of money and attention from the government. The *Sputnik* launch shocked the country into understanding that America had to pay more attention to scientific and technological research, but in 1960 the space effort was still underfunded and understaffed. In his inaugural address and his first state of the union message, Kennedy pledged to help the United States catch up to the Soviet Union in the space race. He had asked the Soviets to cooperate by invoking ". . . the wonders of science instead of its terrors." He proposed that the two nations cooperate in exploring outer space. The Soviet Union, at the time far ahead in the space race, ignored the offer.

The freedom of that city is not negotiable. We cannot negotiate with those who say, "What's mine is mine and what's yours is negotiable."
—JOHN F. KENNEDY
on Berlin

U.S. astronaut Edwin E. Aldrin takes a "giant leap for mankind" on July 22, 1969, as part of the Apollo 11 mission, the first to land on the moon. Kennedy regarded the advancement of science and space technology as a top priority, and in September 1962 pledged that the United States would put a man on the moon before the end of the decade.

UPI/BETTMANN NEWSPHOTOS

This Soviet satellite model on exhibit in New York City is similar to the *Sputnik* satellite that the Soviets launched in October 1957. The Soviets widened their early lead in the "space race" in 1961, when a cosmonaut (Soviet astronaut) became the first person to orbit the earth.

Vice-president Lyndon Johnson was put in charge of the National Space Council, and funding for space programs increased. Although American work on the space project had resulted in some very solid scientific gains, putting humans into space would do the most for American prestige. In a September 12, 1962, speech at Houston's Rice University, Kennedy pledged that America would put a man on the moon, and return him safely to earth, before the end of the decade.

On May 5, 1961, Alan Shepard made a successful spaceflight but did not orbit the earth. In February of 1962 John Glenn orbited the earth three times. The success of the first U.S. orbital flight was the turning point in the nation's space effort, spurring the United States to even greater technological achievements.

On July 20, 1969, Neil Armstrong became the first human to set foot on the moon; without Kennedy's backing of the space program eight years earlier, it is likely that the first moon landing would not have happened until the mid-1970s, if at all.

The space race was another aspect of the cold war struggle for power that had taken place between the United States and the Soviet Union since the end of World War II. Beginning with the establishment of satellite governments in Eastern Europe after World War II and the success of the communist revolution in China in 1949, the Soviet Union had increased its power and prestige around the globe. The United States had tried to prevent the expansion of Soviet influence through diplomacy, United Nations intervention, and economic aid to anticommunist governments.

The German city of Berlin was the most sensitive issue between the United States and the Soviet Union. After Germany's defeat by the Allies in World War II, the country had been divided into Soviet and Western sectors, but the Soviet Union converted its zones into an ostensibly independent communist state, the German Democratic Republic (known to the West as East Germany). The original capital of Germany, Berlin, remained under the control of Great Britain, France, the United States, and the Soviet Union but lay deep within Soviet-controlled East Germany.

At Cape Canaveral, Florida, Kennedy awards a medal to astronaut John Glenn, Jr., the first American to orbit the earth. In response to Soviet advances in space, Kennedy appointed Vice-president Johnson head of the National Space Council and drastically increased federal spending on science education in the nation's schools.

Soviet premier Nikita Khrushchev and Jacqueline Kennedy attend a concert in Vienna, Austria, in June 1961, where Kennedy and the Soviet leader met to discuss Berlin, Laos, and nuclear disarmament. In many ways Khrushchev got the better of the young president, who left the summit in a state of fatigue and frustration.

In 1948 Soviet leader Joseph Stalin had blockaded Berlin to try to bring it completely under Soviet influence, but the United States responded with a massive airlift of food and supplies into the city. After 321 days Stalin lifted the blockade. At the time, only the United States had nuclear weapons, but the Soviets later developed their own nuclear technology and under Premier Nikita Khrushchev demanded that the Allied occupation of Berlin come to an end. They wanted a "demilitarized free city" — which would mean, in effect, leaving Berlin to the Soviets, who could most easily control it. In 1958 Khrushchev imposed a six-month deadline for the "demilitarization" of West Berlin, a deadline he postponed several times.

One big problem for the Soviets was the almost constant stream of refugees moving from the eastern to the western part of the city. By early 1961 there were almost 4,000 people a week fleeing East Berlin. Many trained professionals and technicians were among the refugees, and the Soviets could not afford to lose them.

Certainly the Berlin question was one of the reasons that Khrushchev offered to meet with Kennedy in the spring of 1961. The meeting was held in Vienna, Austria, on June 3 and 4, 1961. For the first time Kennedy came face to face with the man who led the country that Kennedy called "the adversary."

The two leaders discussed Berlin, Laos, and the prospects for nuclear disarmament, including the informal ban on atmospheric testing of nuclear weapons. Khrushchev took a hard line on Berlin, demanding that the United States sign a treaty making Berlin a free city. After the summit, they issued a statement that said only that they hoped to maintain contact on important questions. Then Khrushchev returned to the Soviet Union, and Kennedy, who had visited France before the summit meeting, flew to London.

Despite his public statements, Kennedy was shaken and angry after the summit meeting. Khrushchev, who was known for his bullying tactics, had rattled the young president somewhat. Peter Lisagor, a reporter for the *Chicago Daily News* who rode on Air Force One with the president, wrote: ". . . they had come face-to-face with the enemy, a cunning, shrewd, clever, earthy, incisive, wild in many ways, face of the enemy, which was Khrushchev, who was unlike anything anybody's ever seen. . . . Kennedy looked kind of tired and a bit used up when we went into London."

Kennedy (left, in front car) reviews U.S. troops and a display of heavy artillery in West Germany on June 25, 1963. Kennedy faced a crisis in 1961, when the Soviets constructed a wall to divide the two halves of Berlin.

Having seen his son achieve the presidency, Joseph Kennedy smiles proudly, surrounded by his 17 grandchildren, in September 1961. Three months later he suffered a crippling stroke from which he never completely recovered.

In the months following the summit meeting, Khrushchev's public statements about Berlin became more stern and bellicose, and Kennedy called for increased military spending, a greater draft of young men into the armed forces, and more money for civil defense.

On August 13, 1961, just after midnight, East German troops occupied most of the crossing points on the eastern side of the line dividing East and West Berlin. The streets were torn up and a wall of barbed wire and roadblocks was erected. Within a few days the temporary structure was replaced by a wall made of cinderblocks, mortar, and concrete.

Kennedy's Berlin Task Force immediately went to work and drafted a protest for delivery to the Kremlin. Willy Brandt, mayor of West Berlin, appealed to Washington for help, and in response Kennedy sent

Vice-president Johnson and General Lucius Clay to Berlin. More dramatically, he ordered a convoy of 1,500 U.S. troops to move along the Autobahn, the main road from West Germany to Berlin. Kennedy's speechwriter Theodore Sorensen wrote, "It was his most anxious moment during the prolonged Berlin crisis, his first order of American military units into a potential confrontation with Soviet forces." Kennedy feared that a nuclear war was possible.

During the last weekend in August, U.S. and Soviet tanks lined up facing each other across the boundaries between East and West Berlin. On Sunday the Soviet tanks withdrew. The crisis had lessened, but there was still no ready solution in sight. Khrushchev announced at about the same time that the Soviet Union would resume atmospheric testing of nuclear weapons. Although Kennedy did not like atmospheric testing, he announced the resumption of American nuclear tests in the Pacific on March 2, 1962.

The first year of John F. Kennedy's presidency had seen both challenge and promise: he had weathered the Bay of Pigs disaster by accepting responsibility for it, and the confrontation in Berlin had raised his credibility with the world. Although he was still under doctors' supervision for his Addison's disease and his bad back, his family had adapted well to life in the White House. The children brightened the atmosphere considerably. His daughter Caroline often walked her father downstairs to work in the mornings or sat on his lap during his breakfast meetings. His wife was working hard to restore and refurbish the White House while seeing that his leisure time was warm and relaxed. Only one personal tragedy marked the end of his first year in office; just before Christmas in 1961, Joseph Kennedy suffered a stroke while golfing. Kennedy flew to his father's side as soon as he could. Many weeks passed before Joseph could leave the hospital. The stroke had paralyzed his right side and severely impaired his speech. The next years of his life were a constant struggle to learn how to walk and talk again — but by the time he took his first steps, his son John was dead.

> *We must show in West Berlin that we have no intentions of yielding to false Soviet claims or fierce Soviet threats — that we believe history in time will yield a free and united Berlin and a free and united Europe.*
> —JOHN F. KENNEDY

7

The Cuban Missile Crisis

One of America's economic problems in the 1960s was a deficit in the balance of payments, which meant that the country was buying more from foreign nations than it was selling to them. Kennedy was very concerned about this situation from the start, and toward the end of 1961 he began work on one of the major pieces of legislation of his administration: the 1962 Trade Expansion Act. He believed that in order to sell more of our goods abroad, we would have to buy more foreign goods, while at the same time protecting U.S. producers from any losses they might suffer from increased foreign trade. The theory behind the legislation was that if the United States allowed foreign goods to enter the country more cheaply, foreign countries would extend the same courtesy to U.S. goods, thereby increasing our foreign trade. The Trade Expansion Act did have an effect on foreign trade, although, like most economic matters, the effect took a long time to be felt.

He felt neither uplifted nor weighed down by power. . . . He was a strong president primarily because he was a strong man.
—THEODORE SORENSEN
presidential aide,
on Kennedy

The Cuban missile crisis arose in October 1962 when the United States discovered the sites for Soviet offensive nuclear weapons on Cuba. Kennedy's cool handling of the crisis was a triumph for his administration.

The lessons taught by the Bay of Pigs disaster were very apparent in another international problem of 1962; the attempt by Chiang Kai-shek, president of the island of Formosa (or Taiwan), to attack China.

During the 1949 communist revolution in China, Chiang and his supporters had fled to the island of Formosa, off the coast of China, where they proclaimed themselves to be the only legal Chinese government. One of the government's chief goals was to overthrow the communist government in Beijing (Peking) and retake the country. The United States recognized the Formosa government as the true Chinese government and supported Chiang, especially since mainland China was seen as encouraging communist activities in Southeast Asia, particularly in Vietnam. In 1962 the Formosa government took note of problems within mainland China and decided that the time was ripe for an invasion.

Chiang Kai-shek fled China following the success of the communist revolution there in 1949 and led the Nationalist government on the island of Formosa (Taiwan). Although Kennedy recognized the Nationalists as the legitimate Chinese government, he refused to support Chiang's schemes for an invasion of the mainland.

Kennedy and Jawaharlal Nehru, the first prime minister of India, confer on the White House grounds. When China invaded India in October 1962, Nehru asked the United States for assistance. Kennedy agreed to supply airlifts and small weapons but refused to provide direct military aid.

To Kennedy, the scheme seemed another version of the Bay of Pigs: a tiny exile group against a large, well-controlled nation (in this case, one of the largest countries on earth) in an invasion that would only succeed if the United States backed it with full military power — thereby risking a full-scale nuclear war. Kennedy did not believe that Chiang could take over mainland China, even with U.S. help, and he politely declined assistance. Chiang responded by leaking word of the invasion abroad, hoping to embarrass America into helping him. In response to these threats, China deployed a large number of troops along its eastern coast. Kennedy let it be known that the United States would defend Formosa and the nearby Pescadores islands from any attack, and soon Formosa and China backed away from an actual confrontation.

LAUNCH POSITION

Aerial reconnaissance in October 1962 revealed the Soviet intention to place offensive nuclear missiles in Cuba. Kennedy responded with a naval blockade designed to prevent Soviet ships carrying missiles from arriving in Cuba.

A few months later, though, on October 20, 1962, China's previously small raids into India's Himalayan frontier became an invasion. India was the only neutral country in the area. Although India did accept some aid from the Soviet Union, it was also sympathetic to the United States. On October 26, Indian prime minister Jawaharlal Nehru turned to America for help, and the Kennedy administration responded with airlifts of small weapons. Some people in Washington urged the president to provide more direct U.S. aid, but Kennedy stubbornly refused, believing that such increased support would only escalate the conflict, helping neither India, the United States, or the free world.

The Indian invasion ended in a cease-fire, after which the United States and Great Britain agreed to provide India with help in air defense. However, U.S.-China relations continued to be a problem, and Kennedy tried to keep the door open to the possibility of friendlier relations between the two countries.

MISSILE-READY TENTS

MISSILE ERECTORS

All other concerns were quickly overshadowed by a new foreign affairs crisis. On the evening of October 22, 1962, President Kennedy made an announcement that brought the United States to the brink of nuclear war.

Speaking on television from the Oval Office in the White House, President Kennedy told the nation that the Soviet Union had placed offensive missiles on Cuba. He said that the U.S. Navy was blockading Cuba and would stop any ships carrying arms, and he warned the Soviet Union that if any missile was launched from Cuba the United States would treat it as a Soviet attack on the United States and would attack the Soviet Union in return. "Our goal," he said, "is not the victory of might, but the vindication of right."

Although there were not yet nuclear missiles in Cuba, photographic evidence indicated that sites had been constructed for the future delivery of such missiles. The evidence did clearly show the presence of a wide variety of offensive weaponry of Soviet

Kennedy meets with members of his cabinet and other advisers at the White House to discuss the Cuban missile crisis. Both the president (standing at right, head bowed) and his brother Robert consistently rejected suggestions for an immediate military strike against Cuba.

origin, as well as Soviet military personnel. Kennedy's quarantine — as he called it — of Cuba raised the prospect of direct conflict with the Soviet Union. For perhaps the first time in the nuclear age, the possibility of a nuclear confrontation seemed imminent and real to most Americans.

The United States had suspected that the Soviets might place missiles on Cuba since late in 1961, although the Soviets repeatedly asserted that it was not so. As late as October 13, 1962, Soviet ambassador Anatoly Dobrynin assured the United States that the Soviet Union was aware of the danger of shipping offensive weapons to Cuba and would not engage in such action.

Two days later McGeorge Bundy, Kennedy's special assistant for national security affairs, showed the president aerial photographs of a launching site for Soviet missiles being built 50 miles southwest of Havana, the capital of Cuba. Bundy told the president that the missiles were designed to hold nuclear warheads — they were clearly offensive weapons, meant as a threat to the nations of the western hemisphere. The president ordered Bundy to have low-level reconnaissance flights made over Cuba.

Kennedy convened an *ad hoc* group of his closest advisers to discuss responses to the Cuban crisis. The group was known as the ExCom (the Executive Committee of the National Security Council) and was made up of key advisers from the various government departments. Kennedy acted as chairman.

The greatest problem faced by Kennedy and his advisers was that their information did not indicate whether nuclear warheads for the missiles were already in Cuba. Without warheads, the missiles could do little damage, but with them, the United States faced the prospect of nuclear retaliation for any steps it might take.

Kennedy knew that when the country learned about the Cuban missiles, some people might panic. He tried to keep the crisis secret until he and the ExCom had decided how to handle it. He did not change his schedule, and he ordered his advisers to do the same. The ExCom often met late at night and in various places around Washington, D.C. When they could, they worked around the clock, sleeping on cots set up in their offices. After the first few meetings, Kennedy gave the chairmanship to Robert Kennedy so that he could keep the travel plans he had made before the crisis started.

Some ExCom members, especially those from the military, advocated immediately bombing the missile bases and all Cuban airfields and radar bases, believing that the Soviets did not care enough about Cuba to risk war over it. The president and his brother disagreed with this. Robert Kennedy said: "I can't see letting my brother . . . make an unannounced Pearl Harbor attack on a little country." He also said that the United States was "fighting for something more than just survival" and that "all our heritage and our ideals would be repugnant to such a sneak military attack."

Adlai Stevenson, who served as Kennedy's ambassador to the United Nations, proposed another solution: if the Soviets removed their missiles from Cuba, the United States would give up Guantanamo, its only military base in Cuba, and would take its own missiles out of bases in Turkey. The president did not agree with this either, saying the world would think that the U.S. had been frightened by the missiles on Cuba.

Kennedy wanted to blockade Cuba: surround the island with a line of American navy ships and turn back any ship carrying offensive weapons. He believed that a blockade would give Khrushchev a chance to consider the situation and choose his own course of action, while a military strike at Cuba might force Khrushchev into attacking the United States. Kennedy knew that such an attack might trigger a third world war, but many of his advisers still insisted that the best thing to do was bomb or invade Cuba immediately, which he felt was sure to escalate into a further confrontation.

In the meantime, the U.S. military was put on alert. Strategic Air Command (the air-based portion of the U.S. nuclear defense system) planes took to the skies, military divisions prepared for a possible invasion of Cuba, and American civilians were evacuated from Guantanamo. People began to realize that something important was happening, but except for the ExCom, nobody knew what it was.

Kennedy realized he was facing his greatest challenge. He had earned a reputation for his coolness under fire, but observers noted that it was evident at the time of the ExCom meetings that he was feeling the burden of the decisions he had to make. A misstep or miscalculation could mean nuclear war. He told David Powers: "If it weren't for the children, it would be so easy to press the button! Not just John and Caroline and not just the children in America, but children all over the world who will suffer and die for the decision I have to make."

On Friday, October 19, Kennedy had to leave Washington on a speaking tour. Before he left, he asked his brother and Theodore Sorensen, his close associate and speechwriter, to try to make the ExCom agree on a course of action. He was afraid that further disagreements and delays would prevent him from making the best decision.

On Saturday morning, Robert called his brother in Chicago with bad news: the ExCom could not come to any agreement, and the president would have to fly home immediately. Kennedy announced that he had a cold and returned to Washington.

Eleven ExCom members were in favor of a blockade, while six favored military action. It was clear that the ExCom would never be in agreement, and the situation was getting more urgent. Kennedy decided to blockade Cuba.

He had told his wife about the crisis, and now he suggested that she might want to take Caroline and John away from Washington to a safer place. Jackie decided to stay beside her husband. The next morning, high-ranking messengers were sent to tell the nation's allies about the proposed blockade.

U.S. warships patrol the Caribbean Sea as part of the U.S. blockade of Cuba, October 22, 1962. After five tense days, Khrushchev agreed to withdraw the Soviet missiles in exchange for U.S. assurances that it would not invade Cuba.

Kennedy reports on the Cuban missile crisis at a November press conference. The nation breathed a sigh of relief as the president explained that the Soviet missile bases in Cuba would be dismantled and that arrangements were being made for verification through inspection of the sites.

By now, the United States knew that it was in the middle of a crisis, although the details were still unclear. One hundred eighty U.S. ships surrounded Cuba, and a bomber force, loaded with nuclear weapons, took to the air. U.S. military forces were on alert all over the world. It was possible that Soviet ships might not simply turn back when they reached the blockade, or let themselves be boarded (for inspection to see if they carried weapons), and it was possible that an invasion or air strike might still be necessary. The president met with congressional leaders to explain this before he went on the air Monday night. Many were displeased, but Kennedy believed that he had chosen the best course.

One week after Bundy had presented him with the photographs of the Soviet equipment, the president told the nation about the Cuban missile crisis and announced the blockade. Robert Kennedy later said: "We went to bed that night filled with concern and trepidation, but filled also with a sense of pride in the strength, the purposefulness, and the courage of the president of the United States."

Tuesday, October 23, was one of the tensest days in American history. A poll showed that while 84 percent of the American people agreed with the president's actions, more than half believed that some fighting would result from the blockade, and one in five believed that the nation was facing World War III. People across the country prepared themselves for the worst.

Dobrynin continued to insist that there were no nuclear missiles in Cuba. (He would later maintain that he had been misled by his own government.) While the reconnaissance photographs could not prove that nuclear warheads had arrived on the island, it was believed that some of the Soviet ships sailing to Cuba might be carrying such warheads. The ExCom was informed that morning that many coded messages were traveling between the Soviet Union and Soviet ships headed toward Cuba and that Russian submarines were on their way to the Caribbean. Twenty-five ships were headed directly toward the blockade.

The first Soviet ship entered the blockade zone, then turned around and went back. Fourteen ships stopped or turned back that day. The ones that did not were tankers or passenger ships. Deciding that they were not carrying anything dangerous, Kennedy allowed them through.

Kennedy and Khrushchev communicated almost daily during the crisis. On Friday, October 26, President Kennedy ordered that one ship be boarded, and when nothing was found, he allowed it to proceed; he wanted to let Khrushchev know that the blockade was more than show. But the missile bases were still on Cuba, and more were being built. Neither side wanted war, but nothing could be resolved until the missiles were gone.

> *The cost of freedom is always high, but Americans have always paid it. And one path we shall never choose, and that is the path of surrender or submission.*
> —JOHN F. KENNEDY
> speech announcing the blockade of Cuba,
> Oct. 22, 1962

Soviet ambassador to the United States Anatoly Dobrynin and Kennedy were all smiles in March 1962, before the U.S. discovered that the Soviets were preparing to install offensive weapons in Cuba. Dobrynin repeatedly denied that the Soviets had any such intentions.

The first break came on Friday, October 26, when some high-ranking Soviet diplomats suggested that the Soviet Union would remove its missiles in return for a promise that the United States would not invade Cuba. (In the wake of the Bay of Pigs operation, Cuba remained fearful of U.S. attempts to overthrow the Castro regime and had requested greater protection from the Soviet Union.) Then Khrushchev sent a long, personal cable to Kennedy, which repeated the suggestion and also said: "We and you ought not now to pull on the ends of a rope in which you have tied the knot of war, because the more we pull, the tighter the knot will be tied. . . . Let us not only relax the forces pulling on the ends of the rope; let us take measures to untie that knot. We are ready for this."

However, the message was followed by a second, more negative cable. Soviet diplomats in New York

began destroying sensitive documents, and a U.S. pilot flying over Cuba was shot down and killed. It seemed once again that a military strike against the missile site might be the only solution.

Then the president hesitated. He thought that Khrushchev might be under pressure from his own generals, who were probably also pushing for a military solution. Robert Kennedy's suggestion that the United States ignore Khrushchev's second message and respond only to the first message was taken. Kennedy's response to Khrushchev assured the Soviet Union that the United States would not invade Cuba and reaffirmed the U.S. desire for peace.

The Soviet response arrived early the following morning. Khrushchev accepted Kennedy's terms and would withdraw the missiles from Cuba. The Cuban missile crisis was over, and the immediate threat of nuclear war receded.

MARCH ON WASHINGTON FOR JOBS AND FREEDOM AUGUST 28, 1963

We Shall

Overcome

lomonac

8

Civil Rights

Prior to 1954, segregation — the separation of the races through the use of separate facilities for black and white — had been the rule, if not, in some places, particularly the South, the law of the land. Segregation existed at virtually every level of public life. Blacks had to use separate water fountains, move to the back of the bus, ride in "colored" railroad cars. They could be refused service at restaurants and stores, refused jobs because of their color. There were separate schools for black and white. The worst offenses were in the South, but segregation, discrimination, and racial prejudice existed throughout the United States.

In 1954 the Supreme Court had ordered the desegregation of public schools, but white resistance ran high and enforcing the order was slow. In the early '60s, the Louisiana State Legislature refused to pay teachers in New Orleans public schools for teaching integrated classes; officials closed down the public schools of Prince Edward County, Virginia, rather than desegregate.

> *I ask you to look into your hearts . . . for the one plain, proud, and precious quality that unites all Americans: a sense of justice.*
> —JOHN F. KENNEDY
> on submitting the civil rights bill to Congress, June 19, 1963

The official poster of the civil rights march on Washington, D.C. Kennedy pledged early support for the civil rights movement; consistently backed desegregation, voting rights, and equal education opportunities for blacks; and introduced sweeping civil rights legislation in June 1963.

COLORED WAITING ROOM
INTRASTATE PASSENGERS

A young black serviceman looks up at a "colored waiting room" sign in an Atlanta, Georgia, train station. Segregation was a fact of life in many parts of the United States in the early 1960s. Nonviolent protests aimed at ending such injustice often met with violent resistance by racist whites.

Voting rights also continued to be abused. Southern blacks were prevented from voting by having to pay poll taxes and by failing literacy tests, which were not required of whites. The registrar of voters in Forest County, Mississippi, was forced by the courts to accept 103 applications from blacks. He disqualified 94 of them, some from college graduates. In many areas, blacks who tried to register were threatened with violence or death.

As Kennedy said first in his initial debate with Nixon during the campaign for the presidency, and again later: "The Negro baby born in America today, regardless of the section of the nation in which he is born, has about one-half as much chance of completing high school as a white baby born in the same place on the same day, one-third as much chance of completing college . . . a life expectancy which is seven years shorter, and the prospects of earning only half as much."

Integration was a very controversial topic in the early 1960s. Some people believed very strongly that blacks and whites should not live, play, travel, work, or learn together, while others simply were not aware of the extent of the problem. Although the liberal sector of the Democratic party had backed integration for a long time, little progress had been made.

Kennedy had promised to support desegregation during his campaign for the presidency. However, Congress, particularly senators and representatives from the South, was not willing to back anything as controversial as laws ending racial segregation. Any overt civil rights legislation Kennedy introduced would likely have been voted down. The attempt would have damaged the chances of other Kennedy legislation, some of which, like his proposal to raise the minimum wage and other social legislation, would also benefit blacks.

During his first two years in office, Kennedy worked for civil rights through "executive action" — things he could do without going through Congress. On the day of his inauguration, he noticed that there were no blacks in the Coast Guard honor guard. He complained about it that night, and by 1962 the Coast Guard Academy had its first black

Freedom riders were integrated groups of blacks and whites who fought racial discrimination by riding nonsegregated buses into the South and attempting to use public facilities there. This bus carrying freedom riders was set ablaze in Anniston, Alabama, by white racists, who attacked the passengers as they disembarked.

student. He made his Cabinet members check their departments for racial balance; over the next two years, the number of blacks serving in high positions increased in most departments. For the first time, blacks served as ambassadors to Europe and not just to Africa. Blacks were appointed U.S. attorneys; the number of black attorneys in the Department of Justice rose from 0 to 70. Kennedy appointed five blacks as federal judges and one, Thurgood Marshall, to the Court of Appeals (the highest level of the federal judiciary below the Supreme Court). He also named the first black woman judge, Marjorie Lawson. He created the President's Committee on Equal Employment Opportunity, which tried to make sure that businesses that worked for the government extended employment opportunities to black and white alike. He pushed for better education and equal voting rights for blacks.

Escorted by federal marshals, James Meredith attempts to become the first black man to register for classes at the University of Mississippi. When segregationists and Mississippi governor Ross Barnett blocked Meredith's entry, Kennedy was forced to send in the National Guard to ensure Meredith's enrollment.

UPI/BETTMANN NEWSPHOTOS

It was not enough. Black Americans were tired of waiting for the freedom that had been promised one hundred years earlier when Abraham Lincoln's Emancipation Proclamation freed them from slavery. Under such leaders as the Reverend Martin Luther King, Jr., blacks began a program of civil disobedience, deliberately riding in the whites-only sections of buses, requesting service in whites-only restaurants, and sitting in the whites-only sections of waiting rooms. Inspired by the work of the Indian leader Mohandas Gandhi, King believed very strongly in nonviolence, and the protesters did not start or engage in any fighting. In early May 1961 two busloads of white and black "freedom riders" left Washington, D.C., for Montgomery, Alabama, under the leadership of James Farmer of the Council for Racial Equality (CORE). Other black groups also sent freedom riders to the South.

The freedom riders simply rode the buses and used the public waiting rooms, without segregating black from white, but they were beaten, jailed, and run out of Southern towns. In Anniston, Alabama, angry residents attacked the Freedom Riders' Greyhound bus, slashing tires and breaking the windows. The mob then fire-bombed the bus, holding the doors closed so that the people inside could not escape. Finally the mob let the passengers out, and beat them as they ran from the burning bus. A nearby hospital refused to treat the injured riders; they had to be taken by armed cars to Birmingham to get medical help. A second bus was also assaulted in Anniston, and an elderly schoolteacher suffered permanent brain damage from a blow on the head. When the second bus reached Birmingham, it was attacked again, and the police refused to help until after the passengers were beaten.

Eventually the freedom riders reached Montgomery, only to face even more violence. It was obvious that something had to be done. Robert Kennedy tried to reason with John Patterson, the governor of Alabama, and other Southern politicians. The president sent a special representative, John Seigenthaler, to Montgomery. Seigenthaler was to help encourage the local government to behave respon-

We can never be satisfied as long as a Negro in Mississippi cannot vote and a Negro in New York believes he has nothing for which to vote.
—REVEREND MARTIN LUTHER KING, JR.

sibly, but while trying to protect a black woman, he was attacked by a mob and beaten unconscious.

The president and his brother then sent in more than 600 deputy federal marshals to restore order, despite the opposition of Governor Patterson. On September 22, 1961, the Interstate Commerce Commission (ICC), which governs all travel between the states, required desegregation of all interstate trains, buses, airlines, airports, and waiting rooms. The freedom riders had won an early victory for equal rights.

Kennedy believed that the two most important civil rights issues were education and voting rights. Under Robert Kennedy, the Justice Department filed numerous lawsuits over school desegregation. The department's first priority was voting rights, since if enough blacks became registered voters they could elect representatives who would work to end segregation. Between 1961 and the summer of 1963, the Justice Department filed 42 lawsuits over voting rights in the South (by contrast the Eisenhower administration had filed a total of ten suits in six years). Behind the scenes, the administration worked with private foundations to help individual blacks register to vote.

This civil rights demonstration in Birmingham, Alabama, in April 1963 began as a nonviolent protest under the leadership of the Reverend Martin Luther King, Jr. The protesters were attacked by the police, and many of the protesters were beaten and jailed. King himself was arrested.

UPI/BETTMANN NEWSPHOTOS

Robert Kennedy and the president discuss Governor Ross Barnett's refusal to comply with a federal court order to allow James Meredith to enroll at the University of Mississippi. Under Robert Kennedy, the Justice Department filed numerous lawsuits over school desegregation and minority voting rights.

These steps were not enough. Civil rights groups pressed Kennedy for legislation that would make discrimination illegal throughout the country. Kennedy hesitated. He knew that a civil rights bill would provoke great anger, both in Congress and throughout the country and was unsure that he possessed sufficient political strength to gain the bill's passage. It was possible that an unsuccessful struggle for a civil rights bill would leave his administration politically weak, less able to successfully govern. In the midst of the international crises he faced, he worried that to ". . . provoke a bitter national controversy without achieving any gain would divide the American people at a time when the international scene required maximum unity."

Then history pushed Kennedy forward again. On January 20, 1961, the day Kennedy became president, a black Air Force veteran named James Meredith had applied for admission to the University of Mississippi, in Oxford, Mississippi. The university had never accepted a black student and turned down Meredith's request. Meredith filed a lawsuit, and in June 1962 a federal appeals court ordered that he be allowed to enroll. Ross Barnett, the governor of Mississippi, refused to comply with the court's order. On September 20, when Meredith

Black demonstrators are hosed by firemen in Birmingham in April 1963. The brutality of the Birmingham police enraged many Americans and spurred Kennedy to submit a comprehensive civil rights bill to Congress. The bill was passed in the summer of 1964.

tried to register, he was met by prosegregation demonstrators and by the governor himself, who refused to let him enter the university.

With the help of a court order, Robert Kennedy persuaded Barnett to allow Meredith to register, but even then Barnett insisted that he "be permitted to stand courageously at the door of the school and yield only when a marshal's gun was pointed at him." The attorney general refused; an angry mob gathered at the college, and it seemed that violence was likely even without Barnett's dramatic plans. It

Governor George Wallace of Alabama (second from left), flanked by state police, bars a Justice Department agent from the University of Alabama auditorium, where the agent sought to enroll two blacks in June 1963. Wallace fought racial integration throughout much of his political career.

was finally arranged that Meredith would register on a Sunday night, when the campus was supposed to be empty and quiet; Kennedy agreed, since otherwise his marshals would have to arrest the governor, which was bound to enrage the mob. On Sunday, September 30, 1962, Kennedy gave a televised address in which he assured the viewers that James Meredith had peacefully entered the school.

As the president spoke, Barnett's state troops disappeared, allowing a huge mob onto the campus to attack the federal marshals. In the fighting many people were seriously injured, and two people died. Kennedy was forced to send in the National Guard to restore order. The next day, James Meredith enrolled at the University of Mississippi.

Then, in early April 1963, blacks under the leadership of Martin Luther King staged a nonviolent protest in Birmingham, Alabama. They were attacked by the police, led by Sheriff Eugene "Bull" Connor. The police used clubs, fire hoses, armored cars, and police dogs, and made mass arrests. King and more than 3,300 protesters, many of them children, were jailed. Black homes and a hotel were bombed. News photographers and television cameras brought the scene into every home in the country. The footage of black women and children being beaten and attacked by police dogs shocked the nation. The violence had a catalytic effect. Theodore Sorensen wrote: "Previously timid Negroes were spurred into action in their own cities. Previously indifferent whites were shocked into sympathy." Kennedy remarked that "The civil rights movement should thank God for Bull Connor. He's helped it as much as Abraham Lincoln."

Martin Luther King and President Johnson shake hands following the signing of the civil rights bill in July 1964, six months after Kennedy's assassination. Of all the strides made toward racial equality in the United States since the 1950s, the civil rights bill was the most significant.

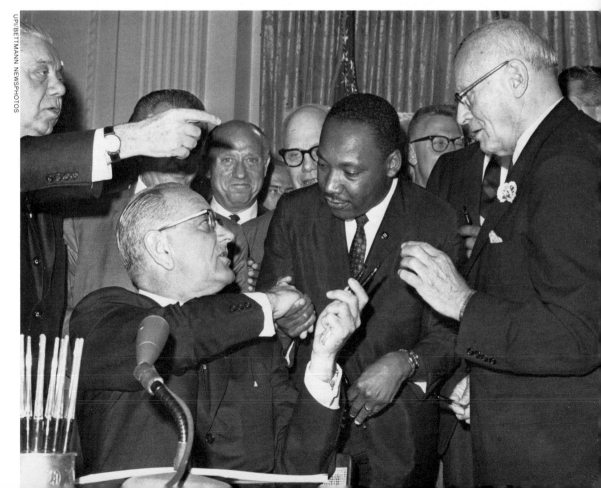

> *Segregation Now —*
> *Segregation Tomorrow —*
> *Segregation Forever!*
> —GEORGE WALLACE
> former governor
> of Alabama

Over the objections of Alabama governor George Wallace, 3,000 troops were sent in to restore order, and the rioting in Birmingham ended. Alabama was also under court pressure to desegregate its schools, but Wallace swore that he would prevent this. Two black students were trying to enroll at the state university, but this time the Kennedy administration was prepared. On June 11, 1963, when Governor Wallace appeared at the university's entrance, the campus was quiet and orderly, despite Wallace's presence.

That night Kennedy went before the American people on television and announced that the time for full racial equality was at hand. He reminded the country that America was founded "on the principle that all men are created equal, and that the rights of every man are diminished when the rights of one man are threatened." He said that America called itself the land of the free, that all citizens were equal, but that what racial discrimination actually said to the world was that "we have no second-class citizens except Negroes; that we have no class or caste system, no ghettos, . . . except . . . for Negroes." He continued ". . . Now the time has come for this nation to fulfill its promise. . . . We face a moral crisis as a country and as a people. It cannot be met by repressive police action. It cannot be left to increased demonstrations in the streets. It cannot be quieted by token moves or talk. It is time to act. . . . A great change is at hand, and our task, our obligation, is to make that revolution, that change, peaceful and constructive for all." In the next week, the president said, he would ask Congress for a full civil rights package.

Although it had been a great speech, and Americans had finally begun to awaken to the necessity for legal action, Kennedy's proposal still stirred great antagonisms. A few hours after his speech, civil rights leader Medgar Evers was killed by a sniper in front of his home in Jackson, Mississippi. The next day a special meeting of Southern senators swore to block any civil rights legislation. The House of Representatives responded by voting down a routine administration bill.

But Kennedy was firmly committed to his course, and on June 19, 1963, he submitted a comprehensive civil rights bill to Congress. He expected it to pass; as Theodore Sorensen said: "He was not interested in a 'moral victory' on a legislative issue — he wanted a legislative victory on a moral issue."

He worked for his bill within Congress and with leaders in labor, education, religion, and industry. These efforts were immediately and surprisingly successful: citizens demanded that Congress pass the bill; segregation signs and practices disappeared from theaters, chain stores, and restaurants. Racial bars to employment began lowering. Of course, this was not true throughout the country. In the South, many white students stayed away from desegregated schools. Wallace tried to prevent

Martin Luther King, Jr., (front, center) leads the March on Washington along Constitution Avenue in August 1963. His famous "I have a dream" speech at the Lincoln Memorial was a passionate declaration of black dreams for freedom and equality in the United States.

black children from entering public schools in Alabama, but he backed down when the president called in the National Guard. Blacks died in Birmingham, including four little girls who died when their church was bombed.

The president had not ended racial inequality in the United States, but the civil rights bill was the greatest step toward that end that the federal government had yet taken. In August, hundreds of

UPI/BETTMANN NEWSPHOTOS

Protesters gather in front of the Washington Monument to listen to speeches and music during the March on Washington, the largest civil rights demonstration in U.S. history. More than 250,000 black and white marchers gathered for the event.

thousands of Americans, black and white, joined together in the "March on Washington" to demonstrate peacefully for civil rights. There, they assembled at the Lincoln Memorial as Reverend King spoke passionately and eloquently of his dream of racial equality and harmony among Americans.

After a long and often bitter struggle, Congress passed Kennedy's civil rights bill in the summer of 1964, six months after Kennedy's assassination.

9

Aftermath

Nineteen sixty-three was a busy year. The U.S. space effort was firmly established and moving forward and the Alliance for Progress was in full swing. Kennedy had taken steps to stop a nationwide railroad strike, had proposed sweeping civil rights reforms, and had signed a nuclear test-ban treaty with the Soviet Union. In June he made a triumphant tour of Europe. In October he further cemented his peace efforts by approving negotiations for the sale of American wheat to the Soviet Union. There was still much to do, and when John F. Kennedy left for Texas on November 21, 1963, he felt confident of the future and ready to lead America into whatever that future had to hold.

He had been president for 1,037 days; beginning his presidency after the quiet, seemingly uneventful years of the Eisenhower administration, he had brought America rushing into the modern world, had sent thousands of young people as ambassadors of peace and progress into undeveloped countries, had faced down the Soviet adversary and then extended a hand of peace toward Moscow.

He knew how to reach people and excite them with hope. Whatever he had, it was real, and it was magic.
—LARRY NEWMAN
on John F. Kennedy

Jacqueline Kennedy and her children, John, Jr., and Caroline, approach the steps of the Capitol on November 24, 1963, to attend a ceremony honoring their late husband and father. They are followed by Robert Kennedy and other family members.

UPI/BETTMANN NEWSPHOTOS

He had not been popular with everyone, but his death rocked the world. Kennedy's brief presidency exuded a sense of optimism and possibility; to many, his death left an unfulfilled promise. Perhaps Arthur M. Schlesinger, jr., a historian and one of his advisers, said it best: "He had so little time . . . yet he had accomplished so much: the new hope for peace on earth, the elimination of nuclear testing in the atmosphere and the abolition of nuclear diplomacy, the new policies toward Latin America and the third world, the reordering of American defense, the emancipation of the American Negro, the revolution in national economic policy, the concern for poverty, the stimulus to the arts, the fight for reason against extremism and mythology. Lifting us be-

John F. Kennedy, the thirty-fifth president of the United States, was the fourth U.S. president to be assassinated. The power of his vision and courage inspired Americans with the belief that they could meet his challenge and build a better, more just society.

UPI/BETTMANN NEWSPHOTOS

UPI/BETTMANN NEWSPHOTOS

yond our capacities, he gave his country back to its best self, wiping away the world's impression of an old nation of old men, weary, played out, fearful of ideas, change and the future; he taught mankind that the process of rediscovering America was not over. He re-established the republic as the first generation of our leaders saw it — young, brave, civilized, rational, gay, tough, questing, exultant in the excitement and potentiality of history. He transformed the American spirit. . . . Above all he gave the world for an imperishable moment the vision of a leader who greatly understood the terror and the hope, the diversity and the possibility, of life on this planet and who made people look beyond nation and race to the future of humanity."

John, Jr., salutes as his father's casket is moved from St. Matthew's Cathedral, Washington, D.C., to Arlington National Cemetery. On the day of Kennedy's funeral, November 25, 1963, Americans shared the family's deep sense of loss as they mourned the death of their president.

Further Reading

Berry, Joseph P. *John F. Kennedy and the Media: The First Television President.* Lanham, MD: University Press of America, 1987.

Burner, David. *The Torch is Passed: The Kennedy Brothers and American Liberalism.* New York: Atheneum, 1984.

Davis, John H. *The Kennedys: Dynasty and Disaster, 1848–1983.* New York: McGraw-Hill, 1984.

Goodwin, Doris Kearns. *The Fitzgeralds and the Kennedys.* New York: Simon & Schuster, 1987.

Hilsman, Roger. *To Move a Nation: The Politics of Foreign Policy in the Administration of John Fitzgerald Kennedy.* New York: Dell, 1987.

Kennedy, John F. *Profiles in Courage.* New York: Harper & Row, 1964.

O'Donnell, Kenneth P., and David F. Powers, with Joseph McCarthy. *Johnny, We Hardly Knew Ye: Memories of John Fitzgerald Kennedy.* Boston: Little, Brown, 1972.

Parmet, Herbert S. *Jack: The Struggles of John F. Kennedy.* New York: Dial, 1980.

———. *JFK: The Presidency of John Fitzgerald Kennedy.* New York: Dial, 1983.

Petrillo, Daniel J. *Robert F. Kennedy.* New York: Chelsea House, 1989.

Schlesinger, Arthur M., jr. *A Thousand Days.* Boston: Houghton Mifflin, 1965.

———. *Robert Kennedy and His Times.* Boston: Houghton Mifflin, 1978.

Sorensen, Theodore C. *The Kennedy Legacy.* New York: Macmillan, 1968.

White, Theodore H. *The Making of the President 1960.* New York: Atheneum, 1962.

Chronology

May 29, 1917	Born John Fitzgerald Kennedy in Brookline, Massachusetts
June 1940	Graduates from Harvard University
July 1940	Publishes *Why England Slept*
Sept. 1941	Enlists in U.S. Navy
Dec. 7, 1941	Japan attacks U.S. naval base at Pearl Harbor; United States officially enters World War II
Aug. 2, 1943	PT 109 destroyed; Kennedy rescues injured crewman
Aug. 12, 1944	Joseph P. Kennedy, Jr., brother, dies while on a secret mission
Nov. 1946	Kennedy elected to the U.S. House of Representatives
1947	Visits Europe and falls ill there; diagnosed as suffering from Addison's disease
1951	Visits Far East
Nov. 1952	Elected to the U.S. Senate
Sept. 12, 1953	Marries Jacqueline Bouvier
1954–55	Nearly dies after back operation; undergoes long convalescence
1957	Caroline Kennedy, daughter, born Kennedy is awarded Pulitzer Prize for *Profiles in Courage*
July 1960	Wins Democratic presidential nomination; gives "New Frontier" speech
Nov. 1960	Elected president of the United States John F. Kennedy, Jr., son, born
March 1961	Kennedy establishes the Peace Corps
April 17, 1961	U.S.-sponsored invasion of Cuba at the Bay of Pigs fails
June 1961	Kennedy meets with Soviet Premier Khrushchev in Vienna
Aug. 1961	Alliance for Progress signed Berlin Wall crisis
March 1962	Kennedy announces resumption of atmospheric nuclear testing
Oct. 1962	Cuban missile crisis
June 1963	Kennedy submits civil rights bill to Congress
Aug. 1963	Signs limited nuclear test-ban treaty with the Soviet Union
Nov. 22, 1963	Assassinated in Dallas, Texas

Index

Addison's disease,   33–34, 43–44
Alliance for Progress,   57, 105
anticommunism,   41–43
appeasement,   25–27
Armstrong, Neil,   69
Barnett, Ross,   96, 97, 98
Batista, Fulgencio,   60
Bay of Pigs invasion,   62–65
Berle, Adolf,   55
Berlin,   69–71, 72–73
Billings, LeMoyne,   27
Birmingham,   99–100, 102
Boston,   22, 30–31
Brahmins,   22
Brandt, Willy,   72
Bundy, McGeorge,   49, 81, 85
Cambodia,   58, 59
Camelot,   15–16, 54
Carter, Jimmy,   18
Castro, Fidel,   60–61, 63, 64
Catholicism, as election issue,   46–47
Central Intelligence Agency (CIA),   60, 62, 63
Chamberlain, Neville,   26, 27
Chiang Kai-shek,   76–77
China,   76–78
Choate Preparatory School,   23, 24, 30
Churchill, Winston,   27, 30
civil rights bill,   95, 101–3
Clay, Lucius,   73
cold war,   41, 69
Connally, John and Nellie,   15, 16
Council for Racial Equality (CORE),   93
Cuba,   14
    Bay of Pigs invasion,   60–65
    missile crisis,   79–87
Cuban Brigade,   61–64
Curley, James,   30
Dallas,   13–17
Democratic National Convention, 1956,
    44–45
desegregation,   91, 101
    freedom riders,   93–94
    school, 89, 94, 101–2
    University of Mississippi,   96–98
Dillon, Douglas,   49
Dobrynin, Anatoly,   80, 85
DOCA (desoxycorticosterone acetate),   34, 44
Donovan, Robert,   28

East Germany (German Democratic Republic),
    69, 70, 72
Eisenhower, Dwight,   37, 38, 43, 44–45, 48,
    61
employment discrimination,   92
Evers, Medgar,   100
ExCom (the Executive Committee of the
    National Security Council),   81, 82,
    83, 85
Farmer, James,   93
Fitzgerald, John ("Honey Fitz"),   23, 30, 31,
    36
Food for Peace Program,   55
Formosa (Taiwan),   76–77
France,   27, 35, 38, 58–59
freedom riders,   93–94
Gagarin, Yuri,   67
Germany see Berlin; East Germany; Nazi
    Germany
Glenn, John,   68
Great Britain,   25–27, 30, 59, 78
Halle, Kay,   33
Harllee, John,   28
Hersey, John,   29
Ho Chi Minh,   58
House of Representatives Un-American
    Activities Committee (HUAC),   41
Humphrey, Hubert,   45
India,   60, 78
Irish immigration,   21–22
Japan,   27, 29
Johnson, Lyndon Baines,   17, 47, 68, 73
Kaysen, Carl,   53
Kefauver, Estes,   45
Kennedy, Bridget Murphy (great-
    grandmother),   22
Kennedy, Caroline (daughter),   50, 73
Kennedy, Edward (brother),   23
Kennedy, Eunice (sister),   23
Kennedy, Jacqueline Bouvier (wife),   13,
    15–16, 17, 39, 45, 50, 54, 62, 73, 83
Kennedy, Jean (sister),   23
Kennedy, John Fitzgerald
    achievements of,   15, 105–7
    advisers of,   48–49
    Alliance for Progress,   57
    assassination of,   13–15, 16–19
    background of,   21–23

Marta Randall is the author of a number of short stories and novels and served two terms as president of the Science Fiction Writers of America. She currently teaches writing and lives in Oakland, California.

Arthur M. Schlesinger, Jr., taught history at Harvard for many years and is currently Albert Schweitzer Professor of the Humanities at City University of New York. He is the author of numerous highly praised works in American history and has twice been awarded the Pulitzer Prize. He served in the White House as special assistant to Presidents Kennedy and Johnson.